My Spiritual Journey

Watchman Nee

Christian Fellowship Publishers

MY SPIRITUAL JOURNEY

ISBN: 978-1-937713-34-8

Available from the Publishers at:
11515 Allecingie Parkway
Richmond, Virginia 23235
www.c-f-p.com

Printed in the United States of America

Contents

Sources Used for the Scripture Quotations

In those excerpts extracted from Watchman Nee's *The Church and the Work* Vol. II and from his *The Normal Christian Life*, the English Revised Version of the Bible (1881-1885) has been used, unless otherwise indicated.

In those excerpts extracted from Watchman Nee's *The Spiritual Man*, the Revised Standard Version of the Bible (1952) has been used, unless otherwise indicated.

The American Standard Version of the Bible (1901) has been used, unless otherwise indicated, in all other excerpts which have been extracted from various other published works of Watchman Nee that are included in the present publication. Likewise, the ASV (1901) has also been used in the Introduction and in the opening introductory sections of both the First and Second Stages.

INTRODUCTION[1]

Spiritual life is pictured in the Holy Scriptures for us as being a heavenly journey. When God delivered the children of Israel out of their bondage in Egypt He led them on a journey to their Promised Land, Canaan. They passed through many stations before they arrived at its eastern border (see Numbers 33). Likewise, we who have received the heavenly calling need to pass through different stages of life before we reach our destination.

Watchman Nee (1903-1972) was raised up by God as His special vessel in China during the twentieth century. Even today his spiritual life influences greatly the saints in China and elsewhere in the Far East. It also has impacted the lives of many saints in the Western world. Under God's sovereign authority he was saved when he was seventeen years of age through the preaching of Dr. Dora Yu who was one of the foremost traveling evangelists in China at that time. Watchman Nee's conversion was so thorough that he took Jesus not only as his Savior but also as his Lord. In his early Christian

---

[1] This introduction has been adapted in translation form from the Introduction which appears in the Chinese-language edition of Watchman Nee's *My Spiritual Journey* (Hong Kong: Found Treasure Publications, 1997). It should be noted that this Hong Kong publication only covers the initial stage of brother Nee's life.—*Translator*

life, the younger Nee was greatly helped by Miss Margaret Barber, a missionary to China.

The deeper the love, the greater the demand. The Lord in His sovereign will dealt with His chosen vessel most strictly. His hand was molding young Watchman who began to learn the lesson of the cross. The heavier the hand of the Lord upon him in stripping and caring for him, the deeper the love of the Lord drew him till he yielded his whole heart to the Lord and loved Him above all things. For nearly ten years the Lord dealt with brother Nee and guided him in walking through what turned out to be a lonely path. Thus was he able to enter practically upon a highly spiritual life—indeed, a self-denying life. Under the constraint of Christ he was able to obey God and live in the environment God had planned for him, and walk in God's appointed way. In fact, he lived under a most difficult environment, faithfully serving God while full of wounds. Thus was God able to pour out through Watchman Nee's life the message of the cross as "rivers of living water" (John 7:38).

Throughout his life brother Nee walked in the way of the cross that was full of praises to the Lord. Though the path was rugged, he could nonetheless sing: "For Your pleasure and glory, Lord, I am willing to bear any cross. I may praise with tears. I have only one prayer: that You may increase and I decrease." Throughout his life as a minister of God Watchman Nee encountered insults as well as praises; and though he was often sorrowful, yet he was always rejoicing (II Corinthians 6:3, 10a). He quietly endured, and out of such life there flowed forth hymns such as the following, whose opening lines read: "The olive, without crushing, yields no oil" (*Christ in Song*, no. 670), "Let me love and not be respected" (*Hymnary*, no. 381), and "Hast thou no scar?" (*Christ in Song*, no. 510). These hymns clearly reveal his spiritual experiences.

There is one matter to which we especially wish to draw the attention of readers. We have no intention to uplift our brother Nee, though we do thank God for him and respect him as a dear servant of the Lord. We do not worship him as some may inadvertently do. For he was a mortal man, having this or that weakness like any other person, and therefore he was not sinless perfect. Yet we do notice how the Lord Jesus, the Perfect Apostle, had molded and fashioned brother Nee, and had tried and disciplined him so that he became in God's hand an apostolic masterpiece of His work. How truly fitting is this Scripture passage from the apostle Paul's writings when considering the life and ministry of Watchman Nee: that God "might make known the riches of his glory upon vessels of mercy, which he afore prepared unto glory, even us, whom he also called" (Romans 9:23-24a). May we be blessed in our earthly lives as much as was brother Nee. In spite of all our weakness we, too, can experience the undeniable fact that "we have this treasure in earthen vessels, that the exceeding greatness of the power may be of God, and not from ourselves" (II Corinthians 4:7).

Most certainly Watchman Nee was one of the vessels that glorified God. During the last stage of his journey he spent the remainder of his life in both prison cell and labor camps. In the second year after the Chinese government changed hands in favor of the Communists, he was informed while in Hong Kong of the difficulty faced by the church back in China. While many were fleeing from China, he himself chose to return to the Chinese mainland. At this same time brother Nee received the sad news of his mother's death. Instead of going to Swatow to bury his mother he asked his sister to take care of the burial arrangements while he himself went straight to Shanghai to take care of the Lord's business. He had not heeded the pleadings of his fellow workers in Hong Kong but went back to Shanghai, knowing full well the danger which lay ahead of him.

In 1952 Watchman Nee was arrested by the Chinese Communist government and was imprisoned and later sent to various labor camps for a total of twenty years. On the verge of his release after completely finishing his term, brother Nee went to be with the Lord whom he so greatly loved on June 1, 1972.

In reviewing Watchman Nee's life one can easily notice four distinctive stages in his spiritual journey. The first stage covers the years from 1920 to 1928: from his regeneration to his basic spiritual training. The second stage covers the years from 1928 to 1942: from the years of the expansion of the work to his withdrawal from ministering. The years of the third stage were those extending from 1942 to 1952: from his withdrawal from ministry to his recovery. The final stage covers the years from 1952 to 1972: from his arrest and imprisonment to his death. All these stages are clearly illustrated by his own words which fortunately have been preserved and were later published. Indeed, this present volume now in the reader's hands has been most appropriately entitled as *My Spiritual Journey*, since every stage in brother Nee's spiritual journey has been described by him either in his writings or else by the words of his spoken ministry.

THE FIRST STAGE OF MY SPIRITUAL JOURNEY (1920-1928)

From Regeneration to Basic Spiritual Training

The first stage of Watchman Nee's spiritual journey, which covers the years 1920 to 1928, commences with his regeneration and includes the basic spiritual learning that he had gone through. He was saved when he was seventeen years of age. Though he was born into a so-called Christian family, he nonetheless showed no interest in Christ Jesus. Not until his mother got saved and apologized to him for her wrong treatment of him did the young Watchman begin to show any real interest in Christianity. He was saved on the evening of the 29th of February 1920. He was alone in his room struggling to decide whether or not to believe in the Lord. He saw the blackness of his sins and the redness of the blood of the Lord Jesus. He yielded himself to Jesus, receiving Him not only as his Savior but also as his Lord. From that time onward brother Nee began to seek the Lord in all earnestness. He spent much time in reading the Bible. He began to witness among his fellow students. He commenced learning the lessons of the cross and went through much suffering. Out of his life experience Watchman Nee learned to know His Lord intimately. Young as he was physically, his spiritual growth was phenomenal. Through his writings we can gain a clear glimpse into his spiritual growth. What follows are a few selections of his writings from this initial stage of his life as remarkable examples of the progress this young disciple of Jesus had already made in his spiritual journey.

1: "MY SPIRITUAL JOURNEY"[2]

Once I dwelt "in the tents of wickedness" (Ps. 84.10), "walked according to the course of this world, according to the prince of the powers of the air, of the spirit that now worketh in the sons of disobedience" (Eph. 2.2), and "lived in the lusts of [my] flesh, doing the desires of the flesh and of the mind, and [was] by nature [a child] of wrath, even as the rest" (Eph. 2.3).

But I then heard "a great high priest, who had passed through the heavens, Jesus the Son of God" (Heb. 4.14) and who is building a mansion for me, for "in my Father's house," He said, there "are many mansions" (John 14.2).

I was once utterly hopeless, just "as it is written, There is none righteous, no, not one; there is none that understandeth, there is none that seeketh after God; they have all turned aside, they are together become unprofitable; there is none that doeth good, no, not so much as one: their throat is an open sepulchre; with their tongues they have used deceit: the poison of asps is under their lips: whose mouth is full of cursing and

---

[2] This essay was written by the author less than two years after his conversion to Christ and was published in Chinese in the December 1921 issue of *Spiritual Light* magazine, a Christian periodical which was then appearing in China. It was much later translated and published in English as Chapter 1 of Part 1 in Watchman Nee, *The Word of the Cross* (New York: Christian Fellowship Publishers, 1995), pp. 3-7.—*Translator*

bitterness: their feet are swift to shed blood; destruction and misery are in their ways; and the way of peace have they not known: there is no fear of God before their eyes. Now we know that what things soever the law saith, it speaketh to them that are under the law; that every mouth may be stopped, and all the world may be brought under the judgment of God" (Rom. 3.10-19). So I made inquiry: "Jesus saith unto them, Believe ye that I am able to do this? They say unto him, Yea, Lord" (Matt. 9.28).

Thus I met Him at "a place called Golgotha, that is to say, The place of a skull" (Matt. 27.33). And what He said to me was: "if thou shalt confess with thy mouth Jesus as Lord, and shalt believe in thy heart that God raised him from the dead, thou shalt be saved: for with the heart man believeth unto righteousness; and with the mouth confession is made unto salvation" (Rom.10.9-10).

Now I am walking as having "purged out the old leaven, that [I] may be a new lump, even as [I am] unleavened. For [my] passover also hath been sacrificed, even Christ" (1 Cor. 5.7). I have "received the gift of the Holy Spirit" (Acts 2.38) who dwells within me.

I today journey in "the way, and the truth, and the life" (John 14.6). I now see God, for "he that hath seen me," said Jesus, "hath seen the Father" (John 14.9).

I found at last the house that I had long sought after—"a building from God, a house not made with hands, eternal in the heavens" (2 Cor. 5.1). This house has but one door, for I see that "by me," declared Jesus, "if any man enter in, he shall be saved" (John 10.9). I now realize the truth of Jesus' saying: "knock, and it shall be opened unto you" (Matt. 7.7).

The house where I today live has a music room—"Glory ye in his holy name: let the heart of them rejoice that seek Jehovah. Seek ye Jehovah and his strength; seek his face evermore" (Ps. 105.3-4). It has a conversation chamber—where I am to "pray without ceasing" (1 Thess. 5.17). It likewise has a reading room—for "examining the scriptures daily, [to see] whether these things were so" (Acts 17.11). And it has a lecture hall—"To the weak I became weak, that I might gain the weak: I am become all things to all men, that I may by all means save some" (1 Cor. 9.22). And finally my bedroom is "Jesus' breast" (John 13.25).

My present lodging is where "I have been crucified with Christ; and it is no longer I that live, but Christ liveth in me: and that life which I now live in the flesh I live in faith, the faith which is in the Son of God, who loved me, and gave himself up for me" (Gal. 2.20). And my address is "in the heavenly places" (Eph. 2.6). Whenever you visit me in the spirit of "Blessed is the man that heareth me [that is, heareth Wisdom, which is Christ], watching daily at my gates, waiting at the posts of my doors" (Prov. 8.34), you will find not only me but also my fellow saints. Take heed to what the servant says, "Come; for all things are now ready" (Luke 14.17).

"Then we that are alive, that are left, shall together with them be caught up in the clouds, to meet the Lord in the air: and so shall we ever be with the Lord" (1 Thess. 4.17). After these words are fulfilled, I shall have my home where "I saw thrones, and they sat upon them: and I saw the souls of them that had been beheaded for the testimony of Jesus, and for the word of God, and such as worshipped not the beast, neither his image, and received not the mark upon their forehead and upon their hand; and they lived, and reigned with Christ a thousand years. The rest of the dead lived not until the thousand years should be finished. This is the first resurrection. Blessed and holy is he that hath part in the first resurrection: over these the second death hath no power; but they shall be priests of God and of Christ, and shall reign with him a thousand years" (Rev. 20.4-6). And the song I sing shall be ". . . a new song, saying, Worthy art thou to take the book, and to open the seals thereof: for thou wast slain, and did purchase unto God with thy blood men of every tribe, and tongue, and people, and nation" (Rev. 5.9).

Not very long afterwards I along with my beloved ones shall move into "a new heaven and a new earth: for the first heaven and the first earth are passed away; and the sea is no more" (Rev. 21.1). For "according to his promise, we look for new heavens and a new earth, wherein dwelleth righteousness" (2 Peter 3.13). "Wherefore," at that time, the word—"if any man is in Christ, he is a new creature: the old things are passed away; behold, they are become new" (2 Cor. 5.17)—shall be fully realized, and I shall gloriously experience the truth of this word: "Rejoice in the Lord always: again I will say, Rejoice" (Phil. 4.4).

In such manner had the saints of old made their own spiritual journey. Yet these lines also represent what I myself have experienced and earnestly expect. Indeed, in writing the very last section, I was beside myself with joyful tears. But I suppose you who are saved have the same feeling towards the return of the Lord Jesus. Those who are cleansed by the blood of Jesus are naturally optimistic towards life. But where will you who have not the assurance of being saved spend eternal death? Please consider!

2: "MUSINGS UNDER THE CROSS"[3]

1. It has not been long since I believed in the Lord [which had occurred on 29 February 1920]. It was only three years and one month ago. There is not much spiritual experience one can talk about, though in God's grace I have been shown a little. I would rather hide this as my personal secret, lest in telling it to people I be misunderstood. For I would suffer painfully should the name of the Lord suffer loss as a result. However, the day of the Lord's return is imminent. The day of us believers returning home is not far away. Will not my fellow travelers have the same feeling as I have? With this in mind and with the Lord's permission, I write this paper to encourage my fellow "strangers and sojourners" in seeking together Christian perfection. What is presented may be taken as some Scripture readings or as fragmentary spiritual experiences (or both). These are but songs sung along the pathway of cross-bearing.

---

[3] These "musings," which the author wrote in Chinese and recorded for himself throughout 1923, first appeared in published form serially in the latter issues (nos. 16-21) of *Spiritual Light* magazine for the year 1923. They were much later translated and published in English as Chapter 2 of Part 1 in Watchman Nee, *The Word of the Cross* (New York: Christian Fellowship Publishers, 1995), pp. 10-30.—*Translator*

"Whom have I in heaven but thee? And there is none upon earth that I desire besides thee" (Ps. 73.25). Last year when I read this, I could not respond heartily. I could not say this word from my heart. This was because my love for my friend was so intense that though I loved the Lord my love was divided. Many times the Lord urged me to forsake all and obey Him, but I could not. Later on He showed me that if I really desired to be greatly used by Him I must fully obey, or else I would not be filled with the Holy Spirit. I tried to bargain with the Lord, saying that having a lover was an excellent thing in life. Why should He insist on my spending this life in loneliness? But He deemed such love as not originating from Him, therefore it was but worldly affection.

February 13th [1923] came. The love of Christ filled my heart, and I surrendered all. I prayed: "O Lord! Hereafter I will not consider myself as mine. For Your sake I am willing to forsake all. I am Yours, be it life or death. O Lord, whom have I in heaven but Thee? And there is none upon earth that I desire besides Thee. The love of Christ is eternal and never fails. Hence, I should love Him forever and ever." Henceforth, each time I think of how the Lord had forsaken all for me, though I too have forsaken all for Him, yet the all I have forsaken for Him is so much less than a millionth of *His* all. O Lord! Keep this consecrated heart of mine.

"Thou didst cause men to ride over our heads" (Ps. 66.12). O Lord! I am open to Your giving others carriage to ride. I am willing to lie in dust and be an unnoticed, unknown servant. Though I be so debased as to have men ride over my head, I am satisfied if only I have You.

"For the help of his countenance" (Ps. 42.5). O Lord! Although lately I have been pressed by circumstances and my future is dark, my course is enlightened by Your smiling face. Even if my whole being is cast down and disquieted, my strength in walking is renewed with just a smile from You. I do not care how people treat me; what I do care about is Your smiling face. All who do the will of God do not lose heart. What other helps do we look for since we already have the Lord's approval and the help of His countenance?

If the thing that I pray for is the Lord's will and He wants me to have it, then He must work towards my having it. In case it is not His will for me to have it, then what use is it for me to even have it?

If I am in the will of the Lord, I must be joyful. If I am not, O Lord, place me in Your will.

"Jesus did not trust himself unto them, for that he knew all men" (John 2.24). God is strong and faithful; I naturally can commit myself to Him. But how about me? Will the Lord commit himself to me? Were I able to know human beings, I would never commit myself to their praises. I only desire the praise from God (see 1 Cor. 4.5).

Valiant men keep the doors (see 1 Chron. 26.1,6-9). The Church of God is in great need of big talents for small uses.

"Jehovah spake . . . saying, . . . he was jealous with my jealousy" (Num. 25.11). On 7 May 1923 I said, "O

Lord, my heart is in sympathy with You. Whatever You are jealous for, I too am jealous. Whatever You love, I also love."

For the sake of Christ, Paul "count[ed] all things to be loss" (Phil. 3.8a). He not only counted all as loss, He actually "suffered the loss of all things" (v.8b). Our offering to the Lord ought not be a lip-offering or a mind-offering; rather, it must be from the heart and factual.

"Paul, a servant of Jesus Christ" (Rom. 1.1). Formerly he was the honor student of Gamaliel, born among a chosen people of God, prominent among the Pharisees, a Roman citizen by right of birth, and having in his hand prized privileges and influence. Later Paul constantly traveled on the road, frequently came down with infirmities, and bore in his body the scars of scourging. He was looked upon by the world as a plague and was despised as "the filth of the world" and "the offscouring of all things" (1 Cor. 4.10). Often he was forsaken and spent his days in desolate loneliness. He was quite familiar with hunger and cold. He worked till dawn making tents. What a Saul he was before: but now he called himself "Paul, a servant of Jesus Christ [the despised Nazarene]." He knew the preciousness of Jesus Christ, for whom he forsook all things.

O Lord! Although I had many opportunities to be Your servant and at the same time have the praise and glory of the world, I would rather be forsaken, going outside the camp to suffer with you [see Heb.13.13].

2. "Suffering" is "glory." Having suffered with the Lord, we shall be glorified with Him. Suffering is future glory; and glory is present suffering.

At first I sought for ease and comfort; but when my love for the Lord became intense I sought for labor. Now I seek neither ease nor labor. If the Lord considers me qualified to suffer a little with Him, then let me suffer according to His good pleasure. I know laboring with the Lord is both joyful and sweet.

I have learned the lesson that in working with people, whatever matter it may be, once an opinion is raised, not to insist any more. If people do not listen, retreat into prayer. Bear all things for Christ's sake. Recall how patient is God. Why can I not be patient too? Let God work out His purpose without my voice.

To the Lord always say "Yes." Whatever the Lord may command me to do, I should say "Yes, Lord." "Not my will but Thy will." This is the secret of victory.

I frequently recall how in past days I was surrounded with earthly friends, and had position, taste and ambition. How great and how lovely it all was! Even now, such recollection tempts me to draw back. "O Lord, enable me for Your sake to forget the things which are behind and stretch forward to the things that are before." [See Phil. 3.13.]

Paul regards us as soldiers of Christ (2 Tim. 2.3-4). When a soldier goes to the front, he is ready to die. If he is wounded, this is no surprise. "O Lord! Make me a believer who counts not life as dear. When my affection is hurt by the world, let me remember that this is expected of believers." It is normal for a soldier to die; it is exceptional for him to live. Why then should we soldiers of Christ be exceptions? A soldier looks for victory; a general is made out of wounds.

In order to serve the Lord, I still remain single. Though I am among men, yet I have been separated from the world. Casting aside my education, forsaking my friends, I travel far and wide beneath the scorching sun to spread the name of the Lord. Rarely do I have sufficient rest and adequate food; I also at times lay by in sick bed. Lacking any help, what do I have except the veiled smile of the Lord's face? On behalf of the Lord, my life here on earth is full of tribulations. During windy mornings and moonlit nights, I cannot help but pity myself if I fall into thinking of myself instead of my Lord. As I recall the past and recount the present, it is hard for me to console myself. Many times I shed tears. "O Lord!" once cried out Peter, "pity thyself" (Matt. 16.22 paraphrased). Jesus in this chapter spoke of going to Jerusalem to suffer. Peter counseled Him with these words, but the Lord judged it as counsel from Satan. "O Lord! From now on deliver me from self-pity. May I never console this useless self. Whether I live or die I am the Lord's. Let me do Thy will to please Thee."

Were you ever alone? Why seek for intimate friends and sigh? Do you not know that in the depth of Jesus' heart there is deep love and unspeakable peace?

O Lord! I am now wholly Yours. Work out Your will in me relentlessly. Have no regard of my discomfort. As long as Your will is done, my heart is satisfied.

O Lord! I am now in need. I gladly accept it so long as this does not disgrace Your name. O my heart, do not be anxious. The Lord knows when is the best time to supply. He is never late. So, rest in Him.

Jesus is the eternal bread. No one both eats the bread and thanks the bread. So let me serve according to the will of God and accept not the praise of men. Let me hide in the Lord. "O Lord! How my heart longs for my home, my country. Come quickly."

I sojourn temporarily in this world. Soon I shall return home—home, sweet home. How joyful is the way to home. Every day I am ready to hear the voice, "Come up hither" (see Rev. 4.1, 11.12). In case misfortune comes upon me, a coffin is enough in sending me to the dust. Even if there be no coffin, what does it matter? Though lonesome on earth, I have the Lord; so I have nothing to be discontented about. Despising the judgment of the world, my heart is satisfied with the Lord's smiling face. "My future is dark, O Lord! Yet with Your one smile it is transformed into light."

Thank the Lord! Today is past, so my homegoing is a day nearer. The coming of the Lord is also a day closer. O Lord Jesus, come quickly.

This morning the Lord calls me to serve Him this day. May the Lord keep me in His love throughout the day and may I be lost to myself.

Formerly I thought my nothingness was a hindrance to God's work; now, though, unless I am nothing I cannot work for Him at all. Hereafter I am an empty vessel in the Lord's hand to be used by Him. Yet even in this regard, Satan subtly comes to work on this nothingness. He tempts me to boast of my nothingness, to make me think of my lackluster nothingness as something to be enjoyed and be proud of! And thus my nothingness is no longer nothing! O Lord, such enjoyment is Satan's counterfeit. May I be abased and the Lord be exalted. May all glory be unto You, Lord. Amen.

3. O Lord! Today two paths lie before me. I do not know which is Yours and which is not Yours. Please show me Your way. O Lord! If I am too big to fit into Your plan, cut me down that I may meet Your will. Or if I am too small to fulfill Your plan, enlarge me that I may accomplish Your purpose.

O Lord! In the past I was a sinner. I thank You, for in Christ Jesus You have forgiven my sins. Make me as holy as You wish me to be.

I am a very sensitive person. Whenever I encounter something, I am either deeply anxious or exceedingly happy over it. Oftentimes I walk to and fro in "Elephant Hill" (that is my temporary earthly address) and commune with the Lord. When I think on my life, I frequently shed tears. If it is not for the Lord, I would not be in such a situation. I love to study. Once I vowed to pursue after the best education I could ever get. And now in order to love my Jesus and serve Him somewhat, I desert my education. How my tears wet my shirt as I reflect on this during my crossing the Ming River. Yet at that time, in view of the pleasant environment and the distinctive love of my Lord, I quickly burst out laughing. "O Lord! I now offer to You both tears and smiles. For my tears and my smiles are Yours. Whether I shed a drop of tear or flash a wink of smile, it is all for You. If Your heart is glad, I am glad and smile. If Your heart is sorrowful, I too am sorrowful and weep." From now on, I am determined not to shed tears over my life situation nor to be joyful over my environment. Whatever may come, I will first enquire where the Lord's heart is and how He will deal with it. "O Lord! Is Your heart joyful? If You are not happy, I too am unhappy. Is Your heart sorrowful? If You are not sorrowful, neither am I."

Last year [1922] came an opportunity for me to go to America to study in the Moody Bible Institute. It stirred my buried wish. It did not happen because it was not the Lord's will. (The will of the Lord is always the best.) This year in July, I traveled with my two friends, Faithful Luke and Simon Meek. When we talked about our mutual friends in America, my heart was again stirred. That very evening I met a lady missionary, and she again invited me to go to the States to study. "O Lord! Now my all is Yours. Whatever you desire of me, that I will do. Whatever You do not want, I will not do. For You I live; for You I die. My hands are on the plow; how, then, dare

I look back at the world? [Luke 9.62] O Lord! I look at You and seek You only."

I wrote on the first page of my Bible, saying that this book speaks of the One whom I have not seen yet love (1 Peter 1.8). Hence I love to read it.

Though Satan may block me, yet he cannot stop me.

Dear reader, is the heavenly path rugged and all ascending? The answer is, Yes. Is it so throughout the days? The answer is, From night to day.

21 October 1923. "O Lord! My heart rejoices. Formerly I rejoiced because I had something to offer You. Today my heart is exceedingly joyful because I have nothing more to offer. And the reason? Because, Lord, all are Yours."

"O Lord! Do I know how to praise You? What I sing is `Your praise'."

"O Lord! Formerly I was satisfied in You, now I know You are my satisfaction. Having You, I want no other person, no other thing, no other event."

"O Lord! Today I am again being misunderstood. I ask You to enable me at this moment to love the person more who misunderstood me. I thank You! For You have never once misunderstood me."

"O precious Lord! It does not matter if people do not love me, for You always love me. People often misjudge my motive, but You always know. Let not people love me unless they love me with Your love."

"My Lord, You always love me! Let nothing stand between You and me. I will come to You, Lord, without interruption, will come to commune with You heart to heart. Worldly affection and glory tend to separate us. May You draw me that I may come closer to You."

On 23 October the Lord said to me: "Unless you count My order as most important, you are not able to save souls for Me." Doing God's will is top priority; saving many souls is not a big issue. "O Lord! Suppose You order me to enter into Your field and labor for ten years without rescuing a single soul; I can be fully contented, for I have done Your will. I want faithfulness, not fruit." Since the Lord apportions the field to me, I will not go elsewhere even if I may save more souls. "O Lord! I will not go to the place of my preference, but go to the field to which You sent me."

4. In the morning of 28 October 1923 I prayed: "O Lord, I now appreciate Your suffering (yet only a tiny bit of it). I went to the country place. I felt nobody knew me. No one sympathized with me. But You came from heaven to earth. Your loneliness, Your solitude ... is beyond description. I now know Your sufferings somewhat. I thank You! For You know my present pains."

The world considers the Lord as the prophet, as Elijah, or as Jeremiah [Matt 16.13-14]. They grossly misunderstand You. "O Lord! How the people misunderstand me . . . O Lord! Henceforth I will never misunderstand You. Whatever You have appointed for me, I will not say, Why, Lord?"

In former days, whenever I received an order from the Lord I considered it too hard, too lonesome for me to fulfill. I even regarded it as an indication that the Lord did not care for me, so He laid such a heavy burden on me. Now I know that all His plans for me are but love. The grace of the Lord Jesus is always sufficient. My past thought of the Lord totally misunderstood Him. "O Lord! From now on, whatever You want me to do and to fulfill, be it suffering or joy, I am willing to accept it from Your loving heart. I dare not misunderstand my beloved Lord anymore. Others may not be satisfied with the Lord; but I am always satisfied with You, and I always love You."

Fat and big fellows deem the road narrow because of their fatness and largeness. Thin and little fellows do not regard the road as narrow because of their thinness and smallness. Jesus spoke of the narrow gate and the straitened way (Matt. 7.13-14). Relatively speaking, so narrow and straitened is this way to the big fellows that they find it hard to walk in it; but to the little fellows they find it easy, for the gate is not so narrow nor the way so straitened to them. The burden of the Lord is light, and His yoke is easy (Matt. 11.30). We should forsake our fat and big "self" to do the Lord's will. "O Lord! I confess to You that when my heart inclines towards self-desire, I judge Your word hard and Your will difficult. But when I wholly seek Your will, I know there is no wider gate and broader way in the whole universe than the will of God." The will of the Lord remains the same. Difficult or easy depends on whether a person inclines to his own will or submits to the Lord's will. May the Lord be my will, and I be nothing.

"O Lord! I know if I go to another place to preach, probably more souls will surrender to You. But, now, because You order me to guard Your border, I dare not move. Here, I am not able to save souls, yet this is Your appointed place for me. I therefore ask You to make me faithful and deliver me from the love of success. Faithful to the thing in hand, faithful to what the Lord has ordained for me. O Lord! Because I love You, I long to see people saved and belong to You. Nevertheless, Your desire is for me to hold the fort. I would rather not save souls that I may please Your heart. O Lord! Your will is the very best. I am willing to obey—to be faithful without seeking for success."

May the Lord take away from me all my earthly friends that I may commune with Him without fluctuation.

"O Lord! Since the world has no love for me and has deserted me, I ask You to protect my loneliness. This solitude in You enables me to have You as my constant companion."

"But thou continuest . . ." (Heb. 1.11-13). O Lord! All are gone; will You go, too? No, "but thou continuest." How undependable are men; You alone are everlasting—lasting ever for me. Thank the Lord!

I sometimes ponder that I have some good but am not loved; I have tribulations but receive no sympathy; I am lonely and poor but am not noticed and cared about.

When I die, there will be no one weeping by my coffin. "O Lord! Do I have to end my life this way?"

"O Lord! I really love You. All that concerns You, I love. I love to hear (hear preaching), I love to read (the Bible), I love to speak (preach), I love to exalt You (praise), I love to converse with You (prayer). I love You because You first loved me."

Let me not be loved by men, because human love may create a misty separation between You and me. I only want Your love, and I love You alone.

You truly are my sufficiency (Gen. 33.9). Having You, I have all things. There will not be any circumstance that I am not happy with.

It is easy to offer to God that which we are able to do. It is hard, however, to offer the heart of offering to God. It is relatively easy to offer up Isaac; but to offer the heart of offering up Isaac, that is, the desire to regain Isaac and let God keep one's heart, that is fairly hard. If this is hard, it proves that we are more concerned with our integrity. We have not died to self. We should not have such a dead-set offering. (The old Chinese proverb says, "Once having mounted, it is hard to dismount.")

"O Lord! I do not desire Your reward; I desire You."

May the Lord help me to maintain a pilgrim's attitude while sojourning on earth. I must never plan to stay here long. I do not know how few are the days I will stay in this day-to-day inn.

It may be today. "I come again, and will receive you unto myself" (John 14.3). What joy!

Having had a picture taken of myself with a few believers, I wrote on the side of the photo: "We know that, if he shall be manifested, we shall be like him" (1 John 3.2). How wonderful!

Many sufferings today for the Lord double future joy.

Today's cross-bearing shall be exchanged for tomorrow's glorious crown. "O Lord! Do You regard me as unworthy to suffer with You? Why is it that no tribulation comes my way this day? Anyway, have Your own will. Do not give me suffering for my sake. Order whatever pleases You."

5. There was a day (in fact, today, 28 December 1923) in which I felt I could not love the Lord. I prayed unceasingly, but I did not sense any love for the Lord. New light came to me. I believe I truly love Him. I praise Him because He loves me. He loves me. He loves me. Wonderful love that loves even me. Now I realize it is not I who love Him; it is He who loves me. Whenever I look within, I see myself and am conscious of how little, if any, I love Him. The more I look at myself, the less I sense my love for Him. But when I look at Him and taste of His love, I am melted in His love. My love for the Lord spontaneously arises. Love the Lord by faith. "O Lord! Although I could not love You, You love me, and so I love You too."

If it were not because of the comfort of the Lord, the affection of the Lord, and the help of the Lord, I would have long been in despair and have died.

"O Lord! Once I entered into Your secret place and was so filled with Your presence. Now I will not be satisfied if my communion with You is but even a few degrees lower than what it was that day."

The Lord's heart is joyful; why should I therefore be anxious? Some say to me: "He who lives by faith uses lots of stamps," which refers to a person using many postal stamps to inform people how he lives by trusting the Lord and how he helps the Lord in His work. This actually is a huge obstacle to faith.

Once a matter is committed to the Lord, it should not be taken back for self-working. The greatest temptation is that after a matter is committed to the Lord, a person reckons that for the Lord to accomplish His work he must spend time to help it be done as though the Lord needs help (see Ps. 37.5). "O Lord! If You desire it for me, You have to bring it to pass. If it is not Your wish, and even though I may be able to work for it, I will not move. Because what I want is Your will."

"O Lord! May the work I do be a self-dying work. Let no one see it except Him whose eye looks from above."

Psalm 88.18: "Lover and friend hast thou put far from me." Some have died, some have departed, some have no knowledge of me. As long as the name of the Lord is praised, what else do I ask for?

"O Lord! Satan and men try to hinder Your work. Will You not intervene while Your little one is placed in such spiritual danger?"

May the love of the Lord be so special to me that I am unable to have my own will on anything.

In former days when I was in trouble, I saw Your faithfulness, and I took You as my bosom friend. Now my sorrow (actually joy) is greatly increased. Worldly friends and Christian associates are all undependable. Misunderstandings many, affections vacillating; but You are different, for You never change. You and I, I and You, are truly joined into one. Now You are really my life. Formerly I could live without You, but now I cannot live for a moment without You.

During December 1923 I was often sick. I felt ashamed in my sickness, for I could not utter the word found in Song of Solomon 5.8, "I am sick from love."

Do not imagine that because you forsake all for the Lord's sake and work for Him, you add glory to Him. Know that the Lord's work is holy work. That He is willing to give His work to you to do is bestowing upon you great grace and honor.

"O Lord! I today desire You yourself more than Your gift as I had done in the past. O Lord! I want You."

"Let others live a peaceful life, having their names on people's lips, all their wishes granted, their influence great, their life full of spiritual power, their work bearing much fruit, and their faith daily increasing; but as for me, I want only the will of God. O Lord, I do not care how You treat others, I only want Your will and want to please You. Your will is the sweetest and the most precious."

Psalm 106.15: "he gave them their request, but sent leanness into their soul." O Lord! I would only ask what the Lord wishes me to ask; do not hear my own prayers.

I now walk faithfully with You step by step till I shall walk into glory.

"O Lord! Not that I crave to serve You more, but that I always long to rejoice Your heart. If Your heart is painful, my tears will flow. What is the use of labor?" (At this point I shed many tears.)

I want to dwell in Your heart, rest on Your breast, and walk in Your path. Nowhere else could gladden Your heart, and neither could it please me.

"I do not love work, neither do I love not to work. I do not seek for my spiritual progress, nor do I seek for my spiritual regress. O Lord! What is Your mind? If You want me to advance spiritually and work, I will advance and work. All is for You, not for me."

"But I said, I have labored in vain, I have spent my strength for nought and vanity; yet surely the justice due to me is with Jehovah, and my recompense with my God. And now saith Jehovah that formed me from the womb to be his servant, to bring Jacob again to him, and that Israel be gathered unto him (for I am honorable in the eyes of Jehovah, and my God is become my strength)" (Is. 49.4-5). This chapter of the Bible speaks of Christ as servant. But we who are fellow servants with the Lord can imitate Him. The words in verses 4 and 5 move my heart. These words are spoken by the servant of the Lord. Christ was sent to save "the lost sheep of the house of Israel" (Matt. 15.24), but He was rejected by the children of Israel. From the human viewpoint Christ seemed to have accomplished nothing. Jehovah sent Him "to bring Jacob again to him," and yet He could not cause "Israel [to] be gathered unto him." Outwardly He had "labored in vain," and had "spent [his] strength for nought and vanity." Yet, Jesus was "obedient even unto death" (Phil. 2.8). He faithfully did the Father's will and denied His own will (see John 5). So that while on earth Jesus was "honorable in the eyes of Jehovah" and "God is become [his] strength."

We all are God's servants. We seek to be faithful to the Father's business, notwithstanding its result. Even if one preaches for ten years without a soul saved, the work is counted as gold, silver and costly stones if it is done in faithful obedience to God. If a work is not done for the Lord but for name and profit (holy name and holy profit)—yea, for the glory of men and the enjoyment of self, then such work is reckoned as wood, hay and stubble (cf. 1 Cor. 3.12ff.). Let it be known that if I am faithful and obedient, and though I may not accomplish anything, I have glory in the eyes of the Lord. It is the Lord who judges. It is His work; therefore, let us not seek men's approval but only His pleasure. The Lord is our all, and we seek nothing but the Lord.

All that is good belongs to the Lord; all that is bad belongs to me.

"Even so let your light shine before men; that they may see your good works, and glorify your Father who is in heaven" (Matt. 5.16). The light shines before men not for the purpose of being seen by men but for the reason that they may glorify God. A beautiful life is not lived for the purpose of being a biography to be read but is for the glory of God. Studying God's word is not for the sake of collecting materials for one's preaching but for the advancement of one's spiritual life. Even the progress in spiritual life is not for the purpose of giving a person more joy but for giving pleasure to the Lord's heart.

"O Lord! I will soon go to the country place to restore my soul. You know my present distress. According to human eyes, my physical weakness has increased, though I am still healthy in You. O Lord! My beloved Lord! Arise and work, or else I will probably go to You before Your return. May the Lord's will be done!"

6. "How dare I withhold anything which may please Your heart? How dare I not surrender absolutely for Your will to be done? O Lord! Please go ahead and work. Your servant quietly waits for Your sending."

"At any time, to any place, for any person, O Lord! May Your will be done."

"Ye put to shame the counsel of the poor, because Jehovah is his refuge" (Ps. 14.6). "Because" in the margin is "but"—"O Lord! What can I say, for having You is all-sufficient for me."

"Without You I do not know how to live. From my youth till now, I always longed to have a friend. Now I have had You!"

"A disciple is not above his teacher, nor a servant above his lord" (see Matt. 10.24-25). Do not ever imagine to have no suffering in this world. Whenever suffering comes, ask the question—How is this suffering to be compared with the Lord's?

"No one knoweth the Son, save the Father" (Matt. 11.27). O Lord! How lonely You were! You were satisfied with doing the Father's will. How can I be discontented since I have You who know me?

We often think about how we can repay the Lord; we therefore rarely praise Him. The more we realize how *impossible* it is for us to reimburse Him, the more we will have the heart and voice of praise, for that is all we can do.

A grain of wheat is beautiful to look at, but it remains a single grain. For this reason, I must not accept the praise of men as though I am able. Like that grain of wheat, let me fall into the ground and die. Let me be hidden in death and be unknown to men. Thus will I, like the fallen grain, bear much fruit. After death, the fruit belongs to the owner of the garden. The dead grain has disappeared. May all glory be to God.

During these months, each time I have taken up my pen to write these "Musings under the Cross," I have written with tears. Now, though, these musings should be concluded. The Lord is coming soon. The sufferings are either passed or will soon be passed. The battle is won, and the victory song is heard. Indeed, this may be the final mile to travel! Very soon I shall meet the Lord and be with Him forever. My feet will not ache anymore.

May our hearts ascend to the heights we have never reached before. May the love of Christ so constrain us that the most beautiful, most admirable, and most glorious things and events and people of this world turn, by comparison, to be detestable. May our blessed hope so fill us that the persecutions, sufferings, misunderstandings and trials of the world become something to be welcomed by us: because they enhance our spiritual progress and set our mind on Jesus. His smiling face and His satisfaction enable us willingly to tread the thorny path. How much easier is this path of ours than the one which He had traveled! May God preserve us through this despicable, dark scene till at last Jesus—our Morning Star—appears (Rev. 22.16).

3: "Beatitudes"[4]

Matthew 5:1-12 are the words that the Lord spoke to His disciples, also to the entire church. Although multitudes were around, these words were not addressed to them. Nevertheless the world also heard them. They realized they could not do them, yet they use these to measure the believers.

"He (Jesus) opened His mouth and taught them" (Matthew 5:2). He had to speak loudly because of the presence of the multitudes. The "them" here refers to His disciples, those who had believed. Since they were now saved, they sought to walk according to the grace that had called them.

"Blessed are the poor in spirit: for theirs is the kingdom of heaven." The Lord pays His first attention to our spiritual life. "Poor in spirit" refers to human nature, to what a person is, not what he does. For God's attention is on what man is, rather than what he has done. For life is far more important than work.

"Poor in spirit" means making no excuse for sin (see Psalm 57:5, 6, 10, 16-17). This has reference to one's humility. (see Isaiah 66: 2).

---

[4] This article, written by the author, appeared in the October 1924 issue of *Revival* magazine—another Christian periodical then appearing in China. It is being translated into English for the first time from the Chinese for this present volume.—*Translator*

"For theirs is the kingdom of heaven." "Kingdom" refers to the millennial kingdom. It means to reign with Christ during the Christ's coming kingdom on earth. For in today's world, they are poor and lonely, yet in the coming age they will be glorious and honorable. They are poor in spirit but rich in Christ. The spirit is always quiet and empty, for aside from the Holy Spirit, there is nothing else in their spirit. This truly is a being poor in spirit. With such spirit, they are able to follow the leading of the Holy Spirit and to have self-control. Thus are the poor in spirit able to reign during the millennium. For the highest comes from the lowest.

"Blessed are they that mourn: for they shall be comforted." Believers bear the cross today, so they are those who mourn. The world seeks happiness as blessing, but how can those who are not of the world be joyful? The world is full of sins. All who can and would be happy in this world must flow with its current or fashion. On the other hand, believers today are pessimistic towards this world, and they are mournful towards a world that rejects Christ. Just as the Lord wept for Jerusalem, so believers weep for this world. Yet they shall be comforted, for the world will not always be the same. One day the Lord shall come and shall establish His millennial reign upon the earth. Then shall the earth be renewed and will not be mourned after. To be any longer mourned in a sinless world would be sin.

"Blessed are the meek: for they shall inherit the earth." What is meant by being "meek"? To be "meek" is to patiently endure unrighteous treatment. Though according to law, unrighteousness can be appealed, one is nevertheless willing to suffer voluntarily. Although the meek one has the power to seek revenge, he accepts such ill-treatment without uttering any word against such evil words and/or threats aimed at him. This sentence in the beatitudes refers to a class of Christians who willingly forfeit their lawful right. Should others invade their freedom, they utter no voice to protect their legal or moral right. They shall therefore inherit the earth for their refusal to seek revenge.

The meek are often driven from their land. Today's land is occupied by those who have money and power. Yet the meek shall ultimately inherit the land.

When do the meek inherit the land? Not now, but in the age to come, that is, during the thousand-year kingdom of Christ. In this present age, they suffer loss and are deprived of earthly joy, wealth and power. They are unable to protect that which they possess, for only the powerful are able to keep their properties. But during the millennial age, the meek shall inherit the earth. For them, today's loss is tomorrow's gain. Hence, let no tomorrow's gain be lost through today's gain.

"Blessed are they that hunger and thirst after righteousness: for they shall be filled." This beatitude does not say "blessed are the righteous"; rather, it says "blessed are they that hunger and thirst after righteousness." Though disciples of Christ are not perfect, for they still retain a sinful nature, they nonetheless seek earnestly after righteousness—after righteous acts—once they have believed the Lord. And they are blessed because they seek to pursue after practical holiness and victory. They are blessed because they seek so earnestly as though hungering and thirsting after food.

"Shall be filled" for "sin shall not have dominion over you" (Romans 6:14) is only partially fulfilled. But at the second coming of the Lord, believers shall have a resurrection body forever without sin and a body whose propensity heretofore had been to sin. At the time of new heavens and new earth, the holy city shall descend with righteousness dwelling in it (see II Peter 3:13).

"Blessed are the merciful: for they shalt obtain mercy." "Merciful" here signifies that if people encroach upon any of our rights or freedom, we have the legitimate right to have punishment meted out upon them; yet, for the sake of being merciful towards them we would rather suffer loss. The word also conveys the thought that whenever people suffer we treat them well. "Merciful" and "righteous" are opposites in meaning. For to be "righteous" is to be mindful of holding onto the loss, without considering the other person's situation. But to be "merciful" is a being willing to forfeit one's lawful right in consideration of the other party's suffering under the demand of law. Since believers are saved through the mercy of God, they ought to show mercy to others.

In the future, all believers will stand before the judgment seat of Christ. At that time, whoever has been merciful on earth shall receive mercy from the Lord (see Psalm 18:25). This, however, does not mean that those who are not merciful will not be saved. It only means that they shall be blamed before the righteous judgment of the Lord; and thus they shall be barred from exercising authority in the millennial kingdom.

"Blessed are the pure in heart: for they shall see God." Being "pure in heart" is not the same as being "pure in hand." Though being pure in the actions of the hand is commendable, being pure in heart is far superior.

We read in Hebrews, "Follow after peace with all men, and the sanctification without which no man shall see the Lord" (12:14). When believers meet the Lord before His judgment seat, this in itself will constitute "judgment" for them. With pure in heart they can face the Lord without regret; this is the "reward". To have the presence of the Most High God and to see His holiness, His virtues, even himself, this is the greatest joy. Possibly due to the impurity of the heart some believers will be deprived of such reward. Hence, "Keep thy heart with all diligence; for out of it are the issues of life" (Proverbs 4:23).

"Blessed are the peacemakers: for they shall be called sons of God." Everywhere in the world, even in the church, there are conflicts, thus providing the believers the opportunities to be peacemakers. Believers should have peace within themselves and also be peacemakers. Alas, those who oppose us are unaware of the difficulty of making peace with them— even more so, the difficulty of having or making peace among themselves. When the millennial kingdom shall arrive, the peacemakers shall be called "the sons of God." When believers were born again through the Holy Spirit, they already became sons of God. But the difference here is that to "be called the sons of God" is the receiving of a special honor. People today are striving for honor, but a certain class of believers shall receive this special honor in the coming kingdom age.

"Blessed are they that have been persecuted for righteousness' sake: for theirs is the kingdom of heaven." This refers to those Old Testament saints who had witnessed for God and had suffered persecution for it. "Righteousness" is the foundation of the Law. These saints suffered much tribulation for the sake of keeping God's commandments. And thus, the kingdom shall be their reward (see Luke 13:28-29). Christians should not only suffer for righteousness' sake but suffer even more so for the sake of Christ.

"Blessed are ye when men shall reproach you, and persecute you, and say all manner of evil against you falsely, for my sake. Rejoice and be exceeding glad: for great is your reward in heaven: for so persecuted they the prophets that were before you." Reproach is mentioned, "because for thy sake I have borne reproach; ... for the zeal of thy house hath eaten me up; and the reproaches of them that reproach thee are fallen upon me" (Psalm 69:7, 9). Persecution is likewise mentioned, and this is a reminder of what is found in I Peter: "when ye do well, and suffer for it. Ye shall take it patiently, this is acceptable with God" (2:20b).

It is also a reminder of what Paul has written in II Timothy: "Yea and all that would live godly in Christ Jesus shall suffer persecution" (3:12). All this is experienced for the sake of loving the Lord. Not only will evil words be spoken against believers. Indeed, it is as though evil words and actual persecutions are still inadequate, for things shall be done and said against their honor. For the sake of the Lord, believers are willing to suffer the loss even of their honor. Those evil words are not true but are falsely made up; and not just of one kind but of many kinds. For those believers who are willing to suffer with their Lord, all such evil treatments are to be expected.

Hence, so all is for the Lord who so loved us and gave His all towards us. He loves us and we love Him. We do not feel pained in suffering for Him. On the contrary, we consider such as something sweet. Consider what I Peter 2:20 said, that blessed are they who suffer for the sake of Christ. As we suffer reproach, persecution and evil accusation, we normally would react with anger against injustice or experience sorrow in heart; yet the Lord says, "Rejoice and be exceeding glad," because to suffer for the Lord's sake is glorious, noble and joyous. In the days of the early church the apostles also suffered reproach (Acts 5:28) and persecution (Acts 5:17, 18, 40). Yet the Bible recorded this: "They therefore departed from the presence of the council rejoicing that they were counted worthy to suffer dishonor for the Name" (Acts 5:41). Having faith will naturally be joyful. To suffer for the Lord is joyous because there will be the glory of the kingdom.

Where Comes This Joy?

1. Because there will be reward in heaven. Today we suffer on earth, but in that coming day there will be reward in heaven. This heavenly reward shall be revealed as being a great reward. As we suffer on earth today, so shall we be rewarded in heaven on that coming day of the Lord's return, for "suffering" and "reward" are in direct proportion to each other. Since our Lord says that his reward is great, it must be great beyond our comprehension.

2. Let us rejoice, for the prophets had also been so persecuted. Since the prophets could be comforted by the Lord for their suffering for righteousness' sake, how much more comfort could be ours? If they shall receive the kingdom, should we wonder at ours? Many suffer for the sake of the Lord; as you and I are not alone. Many prophets of old and saints yesterday and today suffer together with us. Are you aware of it? Believers should know that their present lot is not to be great, high, wonderful, powerful, rich and noble; rather, their portion is to suffer with the Lord. Christ today is still being rejected by the world; even some in the church betray Him. If He has yet to reign on earth, how can we in the least reign today?

Though this path may be lowly, lonely, narrow and long, nevertheless, this path leads to glory and reigning. Step by step this path leads to glory. Today we learn to do all things for the Lord, work according to His heart, and suffer His pain and shame: "for I reckon that the sufferings of this present time are not worthy to be compared with the glory which shall be revealed to us-ward" (Romans 8:18).

4: "THE WORD OF THE CROSS"[5]

How commendable it is that in spite of the profusion in recent days of heresies and apostasies trying to wipe out "the word of the cross," there is still a group of zealous believers who hold fast to the cross and propagate the salvation of the cross. Yet what I find in print as well as in the pulpit concerning the word of the cross does not seem to be systematic, and is sometimes oversimplified, thus unable to benefit those young believers very much. Hence, I would write down here that which the Lord has shown me, so that His name may be glorified and His word may prevail. Amen.

"The word of the cross" has neither beginning nor end. It cannot be measured by time. For the Lamb has been slain from the foundation of the world (Rev. 13.8 mg.). The life of a Christian originates from the cross and is perfected by the cross. If a believer is real, he must trust in the cross. The word of the cross and the believer's life are inseparable.

---

[5] This is the initial article of six written by the author on this general theme, the contents of the first five of which he completed writing in late April 1924. These five first appeared in *Spiritual Light* magazine (presumably 1924). All six articles were much later translated and published in English together as Part Two of Watchman Nee's *The Word of the Cross* (New York: Christian Fellowship Publishers, 1995). This first article can be found on pp. 41-52.—*Translator*

The cross is composed of two sides: and these are inseparable. On the one side of the cross is death; on the other side is resurrection. In the natural realm there is a great gap between man's death and life; but in the spiritual realm, death and life are indivisible. "Death" deals with sin, while "life" deals with righteousness. A natural man is not able to know death since he does not even know life. Yet how can the spiritual man know life if he does not know death? Please take note of these two sides of the cross: "death," and "life."

I. The Death Side of the Cross

On the death side, there are again two aspects—namely, "substitution," and "identification" or "co-death." These two aspects gather up all the significance of the words, "the death of the cross."

A. *Substitution*. This aspect speaks of Christ having died for us. He died for sinners. He stood in the place of sinners. Almost all the types in the Old Testament concerning the suffering of the Lord Jesus refer to this aspect. The offering of sacrifices points to the substitutionary death of the Lord Jesus. Nowhere is this more distinctive than in Isaiah 53 where the substitution of the Lord Jesus is mentioned twelve times:

1. "Surely he hath borne our griefs" (v.4).
2. "And carried our sorrows" (v.4).

3. "He was wounded for our transgressions" (v.5).
4. "He was bruised for our iniquities" (v.5).
5. "The chastisement of our peace was upon him" (v.5).
6. "With his stripes we are healed" (v.5).
7. "Jehovah hath laid on him the iniquity of us all" (v.6).
8. "He was cut off out of the land of the living for the transgression of my people" (v.8).
9. "Thou shalt make his soul an offering for sin" (v.10).
10. "He shall bear their iniquities" (v.11).
11. "He [bore] the sin of many" (v.12).
12. "And made intercession for the transgressors" (v.12).

In the New Testament the concept of "substitution" is made even clearer. For the lost, the Lord Jesus came "to give his life a ransom for many" (Matt. 20.28). To shepherd us, He "lay down [his] life for the sheep" (John 10.15). As to the Church, He "purchased [it] with his own blood" (Acts 20.28). "While we were yet weak, in due season Christ died for the ungodly.... While we were yet sinners, Christ died for us" (Rom. 5.6,8). The first stage of the "gospel" is that "Christ died for our sins according to the scriptures" (1 Cor. 15.3). For He is God and He is man, and therefore He "died for all" (2 Cor. 5.14). Because we have sinned, Christ "who knew no sin he [God] made to be sin on our behalf" (2 Cor. 5.21).

"Though he [Christ] was rich, yet for your sakes he became poor" (2 Cor. 8.9). Had we not sinned and been poor, we would not need His death. Unfortunately, we have all sinned; hence the Lord Jesus could not but become sin for us. He died as our substitute on the cross, bearing the penalty of sin.

Christ "having become a curse for us," the result was that He "redeemed us from the curse of the law" and the method was that He "hang[ed] on a tree" (Gal. 3.13). And now "we have our redemption through his blood, the forgiveness of our trespasses" (Eph. 1.7). "Who his own self [and no other] bare our sins [and not his own] in his body upon the tree" (1 Peter 2.24). "Because Christ also suffered for sins once, the righteous for the unrighteous" (1 Peter 3.18). The substitutionary work of Christ is now finished. All who believe in Him shall not perish but have eternal life.

In this aspect of substitution four distinguishing facts are included; namely, (1) that all are sinners; (2) that the wages of sin is death; (3) that the Lord Jesus died for all; and (4) that whosoever believes—that is, receives—the Lord Jesus as Saviour, is exempt from perdition and possesses eternal life. If one's knowledge of the word of the cross has not reached this stage, he is not yet saved. Indeed, what follows below will not profit anyone like that. So that unless a person has first come to the cross and accepted the Lord Jesus who was lifted up as his Saviour, he is not able to advance to the next stage of the word of the cross.

B. *Identification or Co-Death.* Believing in the substitutionary death of Jesus saves us from the penalty of sin. Co-death with Christ delivers us from the power of sin. For in His death on the cross Christ Jesus not only died for sinners but also took sinners with Him to die. He not only died for sin, He also died to sin: not merely bore the penalty of sin, but also destroyed the power of sin. He caused sinners to die to sin as well as to be freed from the recompense of sin: "knowing this, that our old man was crucified with him [the Lord Jesus]" (Rom. 6.6). The word "crucified" in the Greek is a "living" word, for it varies in tense according to the time indicated. Here, it is the aorist tense; that is, it is so used when the moral import is an abiding one, and when time is not in question (see the Bible translation of J. Nelson Darby, his note "k" on Romans 6.6). It is therefore a once and forever form, which means—once done, forever done. Our "old I" has been crucified with the Lord Jesus: it is an eternally completed fact.

In reading the entire Bible we cannot find a single command saying, "Crucify your old man." This is because our co-death with Christ is an accomplished fact. Just as Christ died for sin once and dies no more, so we who once died with Him on the cross need not to be crucified again today. In order to experience this co-death in our life we need only to believe in this fact related to us in Romans 6.6, and not try to exert our strength to put the old man to death. Just as you are saved by believing in the substitutionary death of the Lord Jesus, so you are delivered from sin and have the body of sin done away with by believing your old man was crucified with Him. The reality of "co-death" and substitutionary death" is all obtained through faith.

"Identification" or "co-death" has also two different aspects: (1) upon once believing that the old man has been crucified, there must be a daily living in this co-death with Christ; and (2) there must be a taking up of the cross daily. The first aspect has to do with a perfect fact. Once a believer accepts this fact, he daily maintains this death even amid seeming appearances that the old man is not dead. Thus shall sin have no power over him. The second aspect is somewhat different. It is a daily experience of the cross: for the Lord's sake, the believer will daily forsake his legitimate rights in this world. This thus differs from the first aspect of forsaking sin.

"Substitutionary death" naturally leads to "co-death." "One died for all" and the result was that "therefore all died" (2 Cor. 5.14). The Lord Jesus died for me and I died in the Lord Jesus. Romans 6 develops on this further: (a) "we who died to sin" (v.2); (b) "baptized into his death" (v.3); (c) "through baptism into death" (v.4); and, (d) "united with him in the likeness of his death" (v.5). All these expand on the meaning of "co-death."

This "death" includes various attitudes of the believer: (1) with respect to sin, the Bible says, "Reckon ye also yourselves to be dead unto sin" (Rom. 6.11); (2)

with respect to the "old I," the Bible says that "our old man was crucified with him, that the body of sin might be done away" (Rom. 6.6); (3) with respect to the law, God's word indicates that with the law comes the knowledge of sin (see Rom 7.7). Sin and the law are closely related. "Ye also were made dead to the law" (Rom. 7.4); (4) with respect to the flesh, the Scriptures say: "they that are of Christ Jesus have crucified the flesh with the passions and the lusts thereof" (Gal. 5.24); (5) with respect to the world, the Scriptures indicate that "through [the cross] the world hath been crucified unto me, and I unto the world" (Gal.6.14); and (6) with respect to the present age, the Bible tells us that if "ye died with Christ from the rudiments of the world, why [are ye] as though living in the world . . . ?" (Col. 2.20) The above six points refer to the attitudes which those who have died with Christ must daily maintain.

What the Lord Jesus said about denying self daily and taking up the cross to follow Him points especially to "suffering" and "shame." For to Him the cross is also shame; indeed, our Lord despised its shame (see Heb. 12.2), but so shall we despise shame too. In Philippians 3.10 Paul noted the same thing: "that I may know ... the fellowship of his sufferings, becoming conformable unto his death."

This kind of co-death is quite different from the six points mentioned before. For this has to do with forfeiting legitimate rights, just as in the example of Christ who "poured out his soul unto death" (Is. 53.12).

"Soul" here comprises man's intellect, feeling and affection. All these are legitimate. Yet our Lord "poured out his soul unto death." In a similar vein Paul said, "I die daily" (1 Cor.15.31).

This stage of life runs parallel to the lesson to be learned in the "life" aspect of the cross (see that discussion below): "we who live are always delivered unto death for Jesus' sake, that the life also of Jesus may be manifested in our mortal flesh" (2 Cor. 4.11). Before we proceed to the "life" side we should daily be delivered unto death for the Lord's sake: die to our environment, die to the world's praise and slander, die to fleshly works, die to words, and die to opinions. Then the life of the Lord Jesus will be manifested and much fruit will be produced (see John 12.24).

"Death" is the believer's passive way with sin, whereas "life" is his active way with righteousness. Without passing through death, life will not come. Passing through death does not require years; it is an act of faith. The moment a person believes in the substitutionary death of the Lord Jesus, at that very moment he believes he receives new life. Many believers are stuck in the "death" position, and thus they are very weak and without power. In their death they fail to experience life. Such believers need also to believe in their life in the Lord Jesus so that they may have the strength to grow.

II. The Life Side of the Cross

The "life" side comprises three aspects; which are, (1) alive with the Lord; (2) the Lord lives in me; and (3) live for the Lord. Upon completing these three aspects, the believer shall live a victorious life. Before proceeding further, however, I must say something so that there will be no misunderstanding. I do not mean that only after people come to the life side do they have life, for when a person believes in the substitutionary death of the Lord Jesus he is born from above with a new life. Through the working together of this new life and the Holy Spirit he is able to believe that the old man was crucified, thus opening the way to the life side. Gradually he advances in the Lord till he attains maturity. We are first made alive together with Christ before we are raised up with Him (see Eph. 2.5- 6).

A. *Alive with the Lord.* In the natural realm, the law of living beings is life before death. But in the spiritual realm it is the reverse; that is to say, death precedes life: "We were buried therefore with him through baptism into death: that like as Christ was raised from the dead through the glory of the Father, so we also might walk in newness of life" (Rom. 6.4). The death of Christ is not a lasting death, since His soul was not left in Hades nor did his body see corruption (see Ps. 16.10); He has risen. Therefore, "if we have become united with him in the likeness of his death, we shall be also in the likeness of his resurrection" (Rom. 6.5).

Although you have not yet tasted the fullness of this new life, you should know that this is God's pronouncement which you must truly believe. You so reckon yourself as dead to sin and "alive unto God in Christ Jesus" (Rom. 6.11). If you have reckoned yourself dead to sin, you should also reckon yourself as alive unto God. As the power of God made Christ live, so the same power makes us live with Christ (see 2 Cor. 13.4). This is a fixed rule: "having been buried with him in baptism, wherein ye were also raised with him through faith in the working of God, who raised him from the dead" (Col. 2.12). Therefore, being raised with the Lord Jesus from the dead is God's fact. It is now only a matter of whether you believe or not. By believing, Christ is already in you.

B. ***The Lord lives in me:*** "always bearing about in the body the dying of Jesus, that the life also of Jesus may be manifested in our body" (2 Cor. 4.10). What is mentioned in A. above is God's fact. Paul believed it, hence here it became his personal spiritual experience. The life of the Lord Jesus Christ dwelt in him and was also manifested through him: "I have been crucified with Christ; and it is no longer I that live, but Christ liveth in me" (Gal. 2.20). Here Paul clearly reckoned as fact that "Christ lives in [him]." Since Christ was his life, he was now filled with Christ as he once was filled with the "old man." Naturally he lived as Christ had lived. This makes a real "Christian."

C. *Live for the Lord.* The length and width and height and depth of the love of Christ is incomprehensible. But with the aforesaid experience one should be able to live for Christ. To live for the Lord is being touched by His love. To live for the Lord is the aftermath of believing in the Lord who laid down His life for all. So Paul continued to declare the following in Galatians 2.20: "that life which I now live in the flesh I live in faith, the faith which is in the Son of God, who loved me, and gave himself up for me." We who are alive in the Lord are so constrained by the immense love of Christ in dying on the cross for us that we will live for Him: "he died for all, that they that live [for through Him believers have been made alive] should no longer live unto themselves, but unto him who for their sakes died and rose again" (2 Cor. 5.15). Whether we live or die, we are the Lord's. Having received the love of Christ, we should declare with Paul: "to me to live is Christ, and to die is gain" (Phil. 1.21).

In reaching this stage in spiritual experience a Christian's life becomes victorious. If one dies daily he lives daily: if one dies to sin he is alive unto the Lord. And he thereby advances to a life of spiritual warfare with Satan. Most Christians today know only the conflict in Romans 7. Who knows that this is but battling with the old man, and therefore such cannot be called spiritual warfare. Spiritual warfare is a wrestling with forces in the spiritual realm, even against Satan and his wicked spirits. Having died and been raised, one's life is hid with Christ in God (see Col. 3.1-3). This is ascension life.

In the Letter to the Ephesians we are told that our life is one of being seated with Christ in the heavenly places (Eph. 2.6), and in chapter 1 it reads, "and made him [the Lord Jesus] to sit at his [the Father's] right hand in the heavenly places, far above all rule, and authority, and power, and dominion [that of Satan and his servants], and every name that is named, not only in this world, but also in that which is to come" (Eph. 1.20-21). Hence our life is now in the heavenly places, and Satan is trodden under our feet. The cross alone gives such victory: "having despoiled the principalities and the powers, he made a show of them openly, triumphing over them in it [the cross]" (Col. 2.15); and, "they overcame him [Satan the accuser] because of the blood of the Lamb" (Rev. 12.11). Hallelujah! Christ is Victor. By His cross we too can overcome Satan and accomplish the Lord's work. Hallelujah!

To help the reader understand, a diagram is given below:

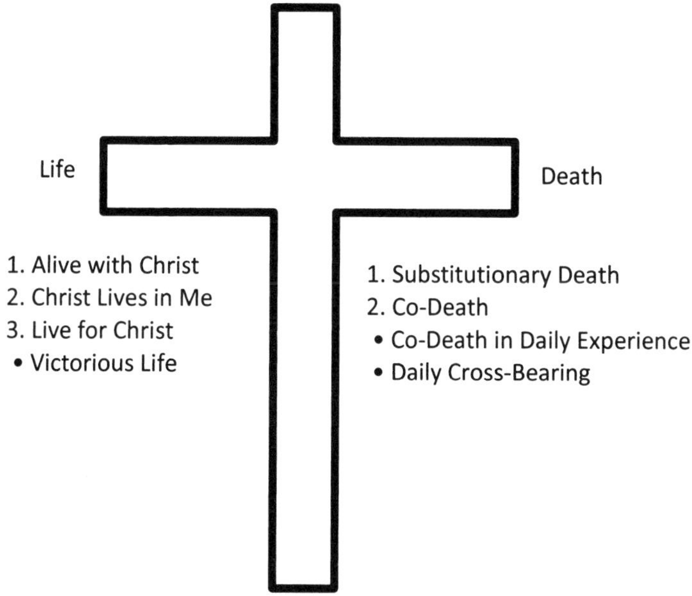

This diagram is drawn according to an understanding of the believer's gradual advance in the word of the cross. It seems to us to be correct according to the light of the Bible. May the reader believe and obey the Christ of the cross. Amen.

5: "Walk in the Will of God"[6]

The reason why so many believers make no progress in their spiritual life is either because they do not walk in God's will or because they do not know how to walk in God's will. They have in their mind so many thoughts—each seeming to be God's will—that they cannot discern what is the right walk. Due to their not walking according to the will of God, their spiritual lives remain stagnant. To those who do not at all seek after God's will, I would beg them to do so. They must not be independent and follow after their own will, for God is our Redeemer who has the right to have us obey His will. Indeed, this is quite proper, whether the matter be viewed from the perspective of rights or from that of love. His great love has so constrained us that we cannot help but seek to do His will.

For those who do not know how to walk in God's will, I would ask you to pay attention to the following considerations.

---

[6] This article was initially a sermon which the author delivered in Chinese at a Friends Revival Meeting presumably sometime in 1924. His text was later revised by the author on 4 November 1924 in preparation for publication as an article, and was subsequently published in *Spiritual Light* magazine. The article was much later translated and published in English as Chapter 10 of Part 1 in Watchman Nee, *Take Heed* (New York: Christian Fellowship Publishers, 1991), pp. 109-130.—*Translator*

(1) We must walk in the *direct* will of God and not in His *permissive* will. The direct will of God is that original mind in the heart of God which He commands us (or guides us) to follow. The permissive will of God, on the other hand, is that which He permits us to do after our (offtimes persistent) entreaties. Let us take the following as an example: The parents see the need one day of an outing for their children. So they take them out for a day. Days later, their children wish to take another trip because they love the beautiful scenery they witnessed the first time. The parents, however, do not see such a need. Yet due to their children's persistent request and their failure to persuade the children otherwise, the parents finally permit them to go out a second time. Here we see that the first outing is the direct will of parents whereas the second outing is their permissive will. Many believers come to God asking—and even insistently so—for permission to do a certain thing, instead of coming to God inquiring if the thing in question is according to His will. This is truly lamentable!

A review of an incident recorded in the Old Testament will help us understand this matter better. In Numbers 22 we learn that the Moabite king, Balak, had sent emissaries to the prophet Balaam inviting him to come and curse the children of Israel. He promised to give the prophet great rewards, which moved the latter's heart (see Jude 11, 2 Peter 2.15). Balaam indeed wanted to go, but having the fear of

God in him, he felt he must ask Jehovah first before any decision was made. "And God said unto Balaam, Thou shalt not go with them; thou shalt not curse the people; for they are blessed" (Num. 22.12). This was unquestionably God's *direct* will. Now after receiving this word from the Lord, Balaam ought to have given up any thought of going. But he told the princes of Balak, "Get you into your land; for Jehovah refuseth to give me leave to go with you" (v.13). How *reluctant in sound* is the word "refuse" that comes from the mouth of the prophet. It was as though Balaam had said to them. "It is not because *I* would not wish to go, but because the Lord does not allow me to go." Whereupon Balak sent princes again to Balaam and promised to promote the latter into great honor. So Balaam came to God once more to ask.

How strange, Balaam! Did not God already tell you on your first approach to Him what His mind and will is? Why do you come to ask the Lord again? Do you think because you are moved by great honor that God too will be so moved? Do you think His will is subject to change? Do you not know that He is the same yesterday, today and forever?

Let us clearly understand here that if Balaam had really wanted to do God's will, he should have frankly told these men on their second visit to him: "God already plainly told me last time that I should not go. So, please return. I will never go." But his greediness so overcame him that he came and entreated Jehovah a second time. Then God said to Balaam: "Rise up, go with them" (v.20). What the Lord meant by His words was: "Since I am not able to restrain you, you may simply go." Which thing the prophet did and went his way.

Now many today do not understand why the angel of Jehovah later came to block Balaam's way to kill him, they not realizing that the way of Balaam was crooked before the Lord (see again 2 Peter 2.15,16 and Num. 22.32b). The same is true in the experience of many Christians today in their walk. They know already in their hearts that the Lord does not want them to do certain things, yet they still love to do them. And whenever opportunities come, therefore, they continue to annoy God by asking. Even though they may not do these things for a time, their hearts have nonetheless already departed from God. And if they eventually do get the Lord's permission, who can question the discipline of the Lord which—as in the case of Balaam with the angel of Jehovah—may follow? For this reason, we must get the Lord's "best," not His "second best." Whoever has a heart that is estranged from God and yet seeks the Lord's will as a cover will be disciplined.

(2) We must not take any text of the Scriptures out of context. The will of God has already been clearly declared in His holy word. All who desire to know the will of God need only search the Scriptures and they shall know His mind on a certain matter. Many believers, however, will simply seize upon one or two verses in the Bible as the will of God for them and act accordingly. They do not seek to know how the whole Bible resolves this problem. This is most dangerous.

Please read Matthew 4.7, which states this: "Jesus said unto him [the devil], Again it is written, Thou shalt not make trial of the Lord thy God." "Again it is written." Again! and again! The devil also quoted Scripture in his temptation of Jesus. Had our Lord been like many believers today, He would have thought that He ought to obey the word of the Scriptures which the Tempter had flung at him. Yet did the Lord Jesus obey? Not at all; for He is one who considers the teaching of the *entire* Scriptures. Hence He answered, "Again it is written." For this reason, in our seeking to know the will of God, we must not pluck a text out of context, randomly choosing and accepting a single verse or passage of verses—in isolation—as the teaching of the Scriptures on a specific issue facing us. We always need to search out whatever other Scripture passages might teach on the particular issue or subject confronting us—that is to say, what *further* words may have been written on it. Let us never make a hasty decision. For just as in the past, the devil today often uses an isolated Scripture verse to deceive men, causing them to listen to lopsided doctrines and to practice many things against the word of God, thus violating His will.

Some believers have a strange way of making a decision—they basing it on a text taken out of context.

They treat the Bible in the fashion of augury. When something happens in their life and they find themselves in a quandary, they will place the Bible before them and pray, "O Lord, I am now about to make a decision on a certain matter, but I do not know if this suits Your will. I will open the Bible at random, and whatever verse my eyes first light upon, this I will take as Your direction for me." Or some may say to God: "I shall open the Bible and whatever verse my finger points at, that shall represent for me Your will." Still others will perhaps say this: "I shall now open the Bible, and the verses which I shall see above (or, below) my eye (or, finger), this I shall take as the Lord's direction." Such a manner of seeking the Lord's will is full of error and quite dangerous to pursue. Satan can easily cause your finger to point at the wrong verse or turn to a wrong page. He has many means and opportunities to ensnare us in his plot. When you ought to stay, he moves you to go. When you should speak, he induces you to be silent.

In conclusion, using the Bible as a means of augury is already out of the will of God. It is very difficult and well-nigh impossible to find the Lord's will through a means that is out of His will. We should never seek to know the will of the Lord in this manner. We ought to spend time daily in the Bible so that we come to understand what it plainly teaches on a certain matter. And thus, when such a matter arises, we will not be at a loss and forced to find a Scripture verse as the Lord's will for us.

(3) Let us never do anything if peace is lacking in our hearts: "Let the peace of Christ rule in your hearts" (Col. 3.15a); "Thou wilt keep him in perfect peace, whose mind is stayed on thee, because he trusteth in thee" (Is. 26.3). When we are confronted with a difficult problem and we do not know how to act in accordance with the will of the Lord, there is a good (though in and of itself not a perfect) way of guidance, which is, to discern if there is peace in our heart. If I do this or that and I have no peace, this shows I should not do it. The word peace here does not simply mean a kind of tranquil feeling. It means that there is an unchanging, proper tranquillity in our spirit. If a thing will cause you to lose the tranquillity of your spirit, it is better for you not to do it. Yet, this is not a perfect means of guidance. Sometimes a thing which ought not to be done gives you peace when you do it and makes you feel unpeaceful if you do not do it. Satan can easily play on our feeling, giving us false peace or false unrest in order to make us do what he wants us to do. Hence, in judging whether or not a matter is God's will, peace is merely a *partial* consideration. We cannot solely depend on it.

(4) Do not look only at environment and need as an indication of God's will. Many in seeking the Lord's will depend on environment as their sole guidance. This will end up in confusion and defeat. Let us look at the story of Jonah. God's will was for His prophet to go to Nineveh, but Jonah decided to go to Tarshish. When he went to the port of Joppa, he indeed found a ship going there. So, he paid the fare and went down into the ship to go to Tarshish (see Jonah 1.3). If the prophet looked solely at environment, he would certainly reckon his escaping from Jehovah as the will of God. Otherwise, how could there have been such a smooth arrangement? In the first part of verse 3 we read: "Jonah rose up to flee unto Tarshish"; and in the next part of the same verse, it states: "and found a ship going to Tarshish." Not only was there a ship going there, it so happened also that he had money in his pocket to pay for the fare. At this time, therefore, the environment was fully in concord with his thought. If a Christian were to find himself in such a situation today, he too would consider himself to be walking in the will of the Lord. Will he not think as follows?—if I go about seeking the will of God in this way, I shall get the approval of my friends and relatives; thus I do not lose human affections and at the same time I can still serve the Lord. I need not spend lots of money and time, and yet the success will be great. The environment is so perfect that I can proceed or stop as I wish. Do not all these factors show that God is leading me?

Let us go back to the story of Jonah. Did he know that he was out of God's will? Let me tell you, there are plenty of ships going to Tarshish. There is sufficient money to pay for the voyage. Nonetheless, neither ship nor cash can guarantee that your trip to Tarshish is correct. For the will of God is for you to go to Nineveh. Hence, in our seeking the Lord's will, we must not look to environment alone, lest we lose our way.

Furthermore, the greatest attraction in environment is need. We may frequently reflect that because there is need in a certain place and because we are able to supply the lack, that that must indeed be the place to which we should go and render help. Suppose, for instance, that I lack some theological education. And suppose, further, that an opportunity is opened to me to provide this lack. If not careful, I might very well interpret this as God's arrangement for me. To take the element of need in environment as their guidance is the common symptom to be found among the majority of believers when it comes to determining the will of God. Their slogan is: "This needs to be done, so I do it." Let us remember, however, that "needs to be done" may not be what God wants you to do.

Let us look at the example of Paul and his companions: "They went through the region of Phrygia and Galatia, having been forbidden of the Holy Spirit to speak the word in Asia; and when they were come over against Mysia, they assayed to go into Bithynia; and the Spirit of Jesus suffered them not" (Acts 16.6-7).

Before the time of verse 6 Paul and his friends had done good works in different places elsewhere. At these places many believers were edified and many sinners were saved. Now they intended to go to Asia (Asia Minor) because the people there seemed to have tremendous needs since many had never heard the gospel that Christ in bearing their sins on the cross had died for sinners such as they. Such great needs among these Asians appeared as though God was leading them to Asia. But no, that was not to be so. The Holy Spirit forbade them to go to Asia. Their thought of going to Bithynia was likely the same, and yet the Spirit of Jesus suffered them not to go there as well. In the light of all this, therefore, it becomes clear that when we seek to know the will of God, we must not depend too much on need that can so easily attract us. For in so doing we may miss the Lord's will.

(5) Do not take the vision or dream as the will of God. Nowadays there are not a few believers in the Church who singularly trust in supernatural phenomena like this as guidance for their actions. They frequently speak of their supernatural experiences, such as when they saw the Lord Jesus and what He said to them; that on a certain night they dreamed of heaven and heard the Lord speak face to face with them regarding what they should do afterwards. Or else that they have had some strange dreams and received such and such interpretations as God's way of directing them to do certain things. Many are the cases like this which can be cited.

Now I do not suggest that all these are false, but I do say that even if these things give us some help we cannot lean on these phenomena alone in knowing the will of God. This is because Satan is quite capable of deceiving believers with false dreams and visions so as to lead them astray from the direct will of God. As a matter of fact I know that many supernatural experiences of many believers are but the disguise of Satan as an angel of light. Not discerning the wiles of the Enemy, God's children end up doing things that do not glorify Him.

We can learn a few things from considering a supernatural experience which the apostle Paul once had. "A vision appeared to Paul in the night: There was a man of Macedonia standing, beseeching him, and saying, Come over into Macedonia, and help us. And when he had seen the vision, straightway we sought to go forth into Macedonia, concluding that God had called us to preach the gospel unto them" (Acts 16.9-10). Now someone may ask, Did not Paul and his fellow-workers decide on the direction of their way by knowing God's will through a vision? The answer is a definite No; for if you read carefully, you will discern that that was just not so. For, first of all, Paul was the only one who saw the vision, yet the decision to go to Macedonia was made by "us." The clear record here is: "*he* [Paul] had seen . . . straightway *we* sought to go."

Their going to Macedonia was not caused by the vision Paul saw. Yes, Paul indeed had a vision, but then he and the others with him were *led of the Lord.* All of them together were of one accord to go to Macedonia. They were not singularly guided by a vision or dream, taking it and it alone as the indication of God's will in the matter. Moreover, the word "concluding" in verse 10 indicates the fact of them all examining the situation before the Lord and deciding together afterwards that God had indeed called them to go and preach the gospel to the Macedonians in Europe.

Hence we see from this that Paul and his companions did not move precipitously merely because of the vision; rather, they weighed the matter very carefully before the Lord in advance of their making the decision to go. In view of this, it ill behooves any of us to rely on these supernatural experiences alone; instead, we should carefully weigh and examine them before the Lord to see if these agree with God's will. Only *then* should any decision be made.

(6) Avoid preconceived ideas lest you fail to receive God's will. One major thing which believers when seeking God's will must avoid is preconception. Having a preconceived notion about anything prevents us from hearing God's voice. "I verily thought with myself," confessed Paul, "that I ought to do many things contrary to the name of Jesus of Nazareth" (Acts 26.9). Such was the preconceived idea which Paul had had of persecuting the church in his unconverted days when he was known as Saul. He did not know the relationship between Moses and the Lord Jesus. He viewed the latter as a great sinner who had perpetrated a great sin against so- called Judaism. So he determined to wipe out this new religion. He went so far as to give his consent to have believers killed and to force them to blaspheme (see Acts 8.1, 26.10-11). He could do all these unrighteous acts with a good conscience. And why? Because he had thought: "I ought." But he had been wrong. Formerly, he had thought that all he had been doing was according to God's will, not realizing it was the very opposite. His mistake lay in his preconception and private idea. Because he conceived what he formerly did as something "ought," therefore he could not receive God's will.

It is highly natural for us to have preconception and personal opinion about matters or about doing things. We cannot forget the persons who hate us or the things we do not like. We are not willing to seek any solution as to God's will by means of a tranquil and restful heart. We always exalt our preconception and private thought, interpreting these to be God's will. Though we may discover our fault later on, it is already too late. Hence, each time we come to God, we must cast aside all our prejudices and ask the Father to guide us. Even if His guidance is totally contrary to the concept we have held earlier, we should gladly follow Him. Never let us plan and decide first, and then pray, using prayer as a pretense and cover.

(7) Do not be hasty, but wait. Some believers are so used to doing things according to their own idea that it is difficult for them to seek and do God's will in all matters, both big and small. They are like wild horses without a bridle, and are thus uncontrollable. They may sometimes appear to be seeking God's will, but before they get an answer from the Lord they have already taken action. How hasty is our flesh in doing things. It deems seeking and following the Lord's will as too slow. When we seek the Lord for His will, we want Him to tell us right away, so that we may commence doing. No doubt our Lord would gladly tell us His will immediately, but for our benefit—because we are yet unready, or because the time has not come—He cannot show us His mind at once. In such circumstances, we must not be hasty, but rather let us wait patiently upon Him. He will reveal His will to us at the proper time.

How sad that in spite of our desire to seek the Lord's will on a certain matter we do not seek to know how to wait. There is a timing involved. If we seek His will but fail to wait for the time He desires to reveal His will, such seeking is false and the result is nil.

In this very connection, let us look closely at an incident from the Old Testament. "He [Saul] tarried seven days, according to the set time that Samuel had appointed: but Samuel came not to Gilgal; and the people were scattered from him. And Saul said, Bring hither the burnt-offering to me, and the peace-offerings. And he offered the burnt-offering. And it came to pass that, as soon as he had made an end of offering the burnt-offering, behold, Samuel came ... And Saul said, Because I saw the people were scattered from me, . . . I forced myself therefore, and offered the burnt-offering. And Samuel said to Saul, Thou hast done foolishly; thou hast not kept the commandment of Jehovah thy God, which he commanded thee: ... but now thy kingdom shall not continue" (1 Sam. 13.8-14a).

Seven days was the time period agreed upon between Samuel and King Saul. Before the seventh day ended, and seeing that Samuel had not arrived, Saul began to offer the burnt-offering. Yet just as he ended the offering, Samuel did come, arriving on time. Saul had rebelled against God's will and was thus reprimanded: and all because he could not wait to the very end. It had appeared to Saul as though Samuel had missed his appointment, so the King began to offer the sacrifice towards the end of the last day. But as soon as he had finished offering, Samuel arrived. Israel's prophet had not broken the agreement; otherwise, how could he have reprimanded King Saul and announced the judgment of God upon him? Saul was denounced because he was too hasty; he could not wait.

Many people act like King Saul. On impulse, they imagine they have to worship God in a certain way, they must arise and do certain work, or they should go to a certain place. So powerful is such inner impulse that they cannot wait but must act straightaway. Do you sometimes feel that a fire is burning within you which drives you to do something at once? You ought to go to sleep, for after a good night's rest, you will find out if such pressure has come from God. Be at rest for a few days. During these few days' quietness God will cause you to understand His will. Let this become a practice in your walk with the Lord. For if such a thought has indeed been injected suddenly in your mind by Satan, it will be calmed down after a good night's sleep or a few days' rest. Let us never act impulsively. Be very sure before any step is taken. Otherwise we too will be reproved by the Lord just as was Saul.

In sum, then, we should wait on the Lord and act only after we have His will. May God protect us from not being able to wait to the last, from not being patient to the end. Let us never "force" ourselves to do anything that we are absolutely certain of, lest we sin against God.

(8) Do not run ahead of the Lord, nor lag behind Him. In this connection, note the following portion of Scripture: "Whenever the cloud was taken up from over the Tent, then after that the children of Israel journeyed: and in the place where the cloud abode, there the children of Israel encamped. At the commandment of Jehovah the children of Israel journeyed, and at the commandment of Jehovah they encamped: as long as the cloud abode upon the tabernacle they remained encamped. And when the cloud tarried upon the tabernacle many days, then the children of Israel kept the charge of Jehovah, and journeyed not. And sometimes the cloud was a few days upon the tabernacle; then according to the commandment of Jehovah they remained encamped, and according to the commandment of Jehovah they journeyed. And sometimes the cloud was from evening until morning; and when the cloud was taken up in the morning, they journeyed: or if it continued by day and by night, when the cloud was taken up, they journeyed. Whether it were two days, or a month, or a year, that the cloud tarried upon the tabernacle, abiding thereon, the children of Israel remained encamped, and journeyed not; but when it was taken up, they journeyed" (Num. 9.17-22).

Here we see a life—a corporate life at that—which obeyed wholly. Whether the Israelites journeyed or remained in camp depended entirely upon Jehovah. With no regard to place or time— whether it were morning, evening, two days, a month or a year—they only followed the will of the Lord. They neither went ahead nor lagged behind Him. They walked in perfect step with their God.

Yet many believers are not like this. Some walk ahead of the Lord. They have entertained many plans and plots and have now already made up their minds. When they contemplate doing a certain thing, they not only decide on *doing* it, they even know *how* to do it. Then they kneel down and pray: "O Lord, we have planned to do a certain thing. Please help us that we may succeed." Though they confess God as Lord, the fact of the matter is that in essence here is how they pray to God: "Hear, my servant! I now have decided on doing a certain thing, but I cannot do it alone. My servant, come and help me!" How sad that many believers treat their God as a servant and know it not. If we are self-centered, it would be better not to ask for the Lord's help lest we make Him our servant. May we not be so self-centered that we walk ahead and therefore ask the Lord to follow.

Some Christians, however, are just the opposite to these who walk ahead. They instead lag far behind the Lord. In whatever matter which the Lord has commanded, they hesitate to proceed. They view fear and excuse as signs of humility. They never finish the course which the Lord has assigned them each day. Such people act like Moses once did—who made many excuses and greatly hesitated to take up responsibility at the time he was called by God (see Ex. 4.1- 17). May the Lord keep us from rushing ahead or lingering behind.

(9) Do not take a prayer answer as the evidence of God's will. Once I asked a Christian, "How do you know this is the will of the Lord?" He said, "Because I have prayed and received an answer." I said, "It is better you do it without prayer." Why? Because what he did was against the Scriptures. Many believers think because they pray and get some sort of response before they act, that what they thereafter do is in conformity to the will of the Lord. This, however, is not so! There is no difference between doing a thing after prayer or doing a thing without prayer (*unless in prayer one really comes to know the will of God*). There are some people who surmise that the first thought or voice that comes *after* prayer must belong to the Lord. They do not know how easily Satan can play his trick on them at that moment and lead them astray. There are other people who fancy that the thought or voice which comes *during* prayer must come from God. How about those wandering and wanton thoughts that sometimes flood our minds during prayer? Can we acknowledge them as coming from God? Of course not! Hence we cannot assume that all which we hear and think during or right after prayer is coming from the Lord.

Some people conclude that a concrete, tangible answer they receive in prayer must surely be the will of God. For instance, I may ask the Lord to open a way for me to do a certain thing. And lo, the way is opened and everything is ready for me to take action. Under such circumstances as these, most of us would likely think that it must certainly be God's will for us to do it. Now sometimes this may indeed be true; nevertheless, this is still not a perfect indication of divine guidance.

Let us take an instance from God's word as an illustration of what has just been said. The children of Israel had lusted exceedingly in the wilderness for meat. The Scriptures tell us this: "he [God] gave them their request, but sent leanness into their soul" (Ps. 106.15). Did not God hear their prayer in this instance? Had He not then performed a great miracle for them that they might have meat to eat? Yet He also sent leanness into their soul, because they were outside of His will to have lusted as they did in their repeated request for meat. How easily they might have mistakenly interpreted the answer to their prayer as proof of their having asked aright in the will of God—that it was indeed His wish to give them meat—yet failing to realize that their leanness of soul was caused by it.

The same could happen to us. Because we pray in the name of the Lord Jesus, we are heard by the Father. But let us here and now be warned lest we consider answered prayer as evidence of our being in the will of God. Sometimes it is better to ask the Lord not to hear our prayer that we may stand firm in His will.

To recapitulate on this point, let us not indiscriminately think that because we have prayed, that because we have received some idea during prayer, or even that because we have had our prayer concretely answered, we can therefore conclude that we must be in God's will. Rather should we seek to know God's will clearly before we make a move. Again let it be reiterated that we are not saying here that answered prayer is totally undependable; not so; yet what we are saying is that we cannot solely depend on it. Other factors need to be taken into account along with answered prayer.

(10) Do not be so stiff-necked or foolish as to wait for the Lord's chastening before knowing His will. Many children of God are frequently out of communion with Him. When their "wild nature" is stirred, they walk according to their own mind. Seeing their wantonness, God is forced to use trial, affliction, even disaster to turn them back. Unless they witness the strong hand of God upon their life, they will not stop proceeding on their own independent way. If, for example, they decide to go somewhere, they will commence their journey without having first ascertained the will of God. They are those who have to wait till they are faced with a mountain without trail or a river without a bridge before they realize that God has not wanted them to go. In doing things they invariably fail to ask the Lord for His will on matters. They will not desist till they meet the heavy hand of God, either in being laid aside sick, in experiencing a surprising lack of funds, or encountering unexpected disaster. Such believers are to be most pitied.

We can use Balaam and Jonah once again as examples here. Not till he met the angel with the sword drawn did Balaam realize that his trip was not in God's will (see Num. 22.31-34). He thought he could gain fame and wealth by taking this trip to Balak. So, too, in the case of Jonah: not till he was buried in the belly of the great fish did he repent (see Jonah 2). If we possess an instructed heart to seek the Lord's will in all things, we will be saved from many rough and unnecessary encounters in life. How many are the trials, afflictions and sorrows that can thus be avoided! Due to our stubbornness or foolishness, however, these things come our way. Yet let us not think that such behavior and consequences belong only to a certain special group of believers. On the contrary, let us acknowledge that in our own experiences many times we, too, will not desist till God raises His hand against us.

"I will instruct thee and teach thee in the way which thou shalt go: I will counsel thee with mine eye upon thee. Be ye not as the horse, or as the mule, which have no understanding; whose trappings must be bit and bridle to hold them in, else they will not come near unto thee" (Ps. 32.8-9). These two Scripture verses plainly tell us that God's *original* thought is not to instruct us with a strong or heavy hand. He does not want us to be ignorant like the horse or the mule which must be held in with bit and bridle; otherwise, like them, we will not know how to obey. His desire is to have us commune with Him, and through such sweet communion come to know His will and then do it. He promises to guide us with His eye, which means that we ought always to look at Him so as to preclude His having to open His mouth but can counsel us with His eye alone. How wonderful this must be! However, for the Lord to be able to counsel us solely with His eye, we must maintain such communion with Him that as soon as He commands we know instantly and follow immediately. We ought to so wait on Him, look at Him and obey Him that He finds no need to use bit and bridle for getting us to know His will.

CONCLUDING WORDS

The ten points discussed above are the key elements upon which all who desire to walk in the will of the Lord must take special care to ponder. Please notice that in seeking to walk in the Lord's will we need to consider a variety of factors and not depend on but one particular way or method of guidance; otherwise, we shall fail in our attempt. In the event we make any decision before we are very clear of the Lord's will, we should purpose in our heart to stop proceeding or to change our mind as soon as we discover it is not the will of God. But if we already know of the Lord's will, we must not doubt or hesitate but rather press on and obey to the end, in spite of many oppositions or persecutions seemingly waiting to push us down. In so doing, we will discover that the afflictions and oppositions we anticipate are but the volleys lobbed at us by Satan ahead of time. In that case we can view them as empty threatenings; for as we move on in fulfilling the Lord's will they shall all disappear. Then we shall realize how meaningless have been our fears and doubts.

Hence after clearly knowing the Lord's will, we must launch straight ahead and be anxious for nothing. Though on the way there may be many threats, we nonetheless recognize that these are but the roarings of Satan. They cannot hurt anyone. Therefore, brethren, "Arise, and let us go on!"

6: Excerpts from *The Spiritual Man*

[7]To the Lord whom I serve I offer my heartfelt thanks, for He has given me the privilege of writing this book. I had always hoped another more capable would undertake this work, yet it pleases the Lord to call me to it. If the choice were left to me I should be the last of all to write; for I have the least desire to do such a book. My hesitation lies not in withdrawal from duty but rather in the realization that such a book touching on the way of spiritual life and the stratagem of spiritual warfare is surely beyond the possibility of one whose experience of the Lord has been less than ten years long. The Bible does permit a believer to relate his experience; the Holy Spirit even leads one to do so; how much better though if such experiences as "caught up into the third heaven" be mentioned after "fourteen years." Now I do not have a "third heaven" experience, neither have I received

[7] What follows is an excerpt extracted from the author's first of two Prefaces to his lengthy treatise on the spiritual life and warfare of the Christian which he wrote in Chinese during the mid-1920s, with this first Preface having been signed and dated 4 June 1927 and the second, 25 June 1928. Long afterwards the treatise would be translated and published in English in three physical volumes under the title, *The Spiritual Man* (New York: Christian Fellowship Publishers, 1968), reprinted as a Combined Edition, 1977. This first Preface excerpt can be found in Vol. I, pp. 7-9.—*Translator*

great revelation, but I have learned through His grace to follow the Lord in the small things of the day. In this work, therefore, my attempt is but to impart to the children of God that which I have received from the Lord in these years.

It was about four years ago that I felt called to write such a book. At that time I was resting from physical weakness in a small hut by the river, praying and reading the Word. I felt the urgent need for a book—based on the Word and on experience—which would give God's children a clear understanding of spiritual life in order that the Holy Spirit might use it in leading the saints onward and in delivering them from groping in darkness. It was then that I knew I was commissioned by the Lord to undertake this task. I began to compose the chapters which discuss the differentiation of spirit, soul and body, a chapter on the body, and also the first part of the chapter dealing with soul life. But I soon discontinued writing. I had many other claims upon my time besides this one. That was not the main deterrent, however, for I could still find opportunity to write. I lay down my pen chiefly because up to that time many truths were yet to be written which had not been fully proven in my experience. This lack I knew would lessen the value as well as the power of the book. I would prefer to learn more before the Lord and prove His truths through experience. What I wrote would then be spiritual realities instead of merely spiritual theories. Thus the work was suspended for three years.

I can say that during these three years I had the book daily in my heart. Although some might consider the publishing of this work long overdue, I could clearly see the hand of the Lord. Within these few years the truths contained in this book, especially those in the last volume, have liberated many from the power of darkness, demonstrating that we had touched spiritual reality. By the special grace of the Lord I was enabled to understand more of the purpose of God's redemption in dividing the new and the old creations. I praise the Lord for that. The Lord also gave me opportunities to meet many of his choicest ones during my various travels. This increased my observation, knowledge and experience. In my contacts with people the Lord showed me not only what is genuinely lacking among His children but what is the revealed remedy in His Word as well. Let me therefore tell my readers that this is a manual on spiritual life, every point of which can be experimentally proven.

Due to my special experience in the physical body during these few years, it has been given me to know more of the reality of eternity and, likewise, the great debt I owe the church of God. Thus I hoped I would be able to finish this book within a short period. Thanks to God the Father and to some of my friends in the Lord, I was provided with a quiet place for resting and writing. Within a few months I had finished Parts I through IV. Although I have not yet begun the other parts, I am sure

God the Father will supply the necessary grace at the needed time.

[8]Many months have passed since I commenced writing this final portion of the book. I can truthfully say that during these months the burden of this work has been upon me daily. It is natural for the enemy to hate the spreading of God's truth. As a consequence I have been attacked and assaulted incessantly. Thanks be unto God, His grace has hitherto sustained me. Often I thought it would be impossible to continue writing because the pressure upon my spirit was too heavy and the stamina of my body too weak; yea, I even despaired of life itself. As often as I despaired, however, just as often was I strengthened by the God whom I serve, according to His promise and through the prayers of many. Today the task is finished and the burden is discharged. What comfort I now experience!

[9]I desire my readers to understand thoroughly that this work is in no way to be considered a treatise on the theory of spiritual life and warfare. I myself can testify that I have learned these truths through much suffering, trial and failure. It can almost be said that every one of these teachings has been branded with fire. And these words are not used lightly; they come from the depth of

[8] Watchman Nee, *The Spiritual Man*, Second Preface, Vol. I, p. 15.
[9] *Ibid.*, p. 16.

the heart. God knows from whence these truths do come.

[10]The deeper the truth the easier is it to become theoretical. Apart from the working of the Holy Spirit, none can arrive at deeper truth. Thus some will treat these principles as a sort of ideal. Let us therefore be careful lest we accept the teachings in the book with our mind and deceive ourselves into thinking we have possessed them already. This is most dangerous, for deception which comes from the flesh and the evil spirit shall increase day by day.

The reader also should be watchful lest he misuse the knowledge he obtains from these pages to criticize others. It is very easy for us to say this is of the spirit and that is of the flesh; but do we not know we ourselves are no exception? Truth is given to set people free, not to find fault. In criticizing we prove ourselves to be not one bit less soulish or carnal than the criticized. The danger is most serious; consequently we need to exercise great caution.

SPIRIT, SOUL, AND BODY[11]

The ordinary concept of the constitution of human beings is dualistic—soul and body. According to this concept soul is the invisible inner spiritual part, while

---

[10] *Ibid.*, p. 17.
[11] Watchman Nee, *The Spiritual Man*, Vol. I, Part 1, Ch. 1, pp. 21-30.

body is the visible outer corporal part. Though there is some truth to this, it is nevertheless inaccurate. Such an opinion comes from fallen man, not from God; apart from God's revelation, no concept is dependable. That the body is man's outward sheath is undoubtedly correct, but the Bible never confuses spirit and soul as though they are the same. Not only are they different in terms; their very natures differ from each other. The Word of God does not divide man into the two parts of soul and body. It treats man, rather, as tripartite—spirit, soul and body. 1 Thessalonians 5.23 reads: "May the God of peace himself sanctify you wholly; and may your spirit and soul and body be kept sound and blameless at the coming of our Lord Jesus Christ." This verse precisely shows that the whole man is divided into three parts. The Apostle Paul refers here to the complete sanctification of believers, "sanctify you *wholly*." According to the Apostle, how is a person wholly sanctified? By his spirit and soul and body being kept. From this we can easily understand that the whole person comprises these three parts. This verse also makes a distinction between spirit and soul; otherwise, Paul would have said simply "your soul." Since God has distinguished the human spirit from the human soul, we conclude that man is composed of not two, but three, parts: spirit, soul and body.

Is it a matter of any consequence to divide spirit and soul? It is an issue of *supreme* importance for it affects tremendously the spiritual life of a believer. How can a believer understand spiritual life if he does not know what is the extent of the realm of the spirit? Without such understanding how can he grow spiritually? To fail to distinguish between spirit and soul is fatal to spiritual maturity. Christians often account what is soulical as spiritual, and thus they remain in a soulish state and seek not what is really spiritual. How can we escape loss if we confuse what God has divided?

Spiritual knowledge is very important to spiritual life. Let us add, however, that it is equally as, if not more, important for a believer to be humble and willing to accept the teaching of the Holy Spirit. If so, the Holy Spirit will grant him the experience of the dividing of spirit and soul, although he may not have too much knowledge concerning this truth. On the one hand, the most ignorant believer, without the slightest idea of the division of spirit and soul, may yet experience such a dividing in real life. On the other hand, the most informed believer, completely conversant with the truth concerning spirit and soul, may nonetheless have no experience of it. Far better is that person who may have both the knowledge and the experience. The majority, however, lack such experience. Consequently, it is well initially to lead these to know the different functions of spirit and soul and then to encourage them to seek what is spiritual.

Other portions of the Scriptures make this same differentiation between spirit and soul. "For the word of God is living and active, sharper than any two-edged sword, piercing to the division of *soul and spirit,* of joints and marrow, and discerning the thoughts and intentions of the heart" (Heb. 4.12). The writer in this verse divides man's non-corporal elements into two parts, "soul and spirit." The corporal part is mentioned here as including the joints and marrow—organs of motion and sensation. When the priest uses the sword to cut and completely dissect the sacrifice, nothing inside can be hidden. Even joint and marrow are separated. In like manner the Lord Jesus uses the Word of God on His people to separate thoroughly, to pierce even to the division of the spiritual, the soulical, and the physical. And from this it follows that since soul and spirit can be *divided,* they must be different in nature. It is thus evident here that man is a composite of three parts.

The Creation of Man

"And Jehovah God formed man of dust from the ground, and breathed into his nostrils the breath of life; and man became a living soul" (Gen. 2.7 ASV). When God first created man He formed him of dust from the ground, and then breathed "the breath of life" into his nostrils. As soon as the breath of life, which became man's spirit, came into contact with man's body, the soul was produced. Hence the soul is the combination of man's body and spirit. The Scriptures therefore call man "a living soul." The breath of life became man's spirit; that is, the principle of life within him. The Lord Jesus tells us "it is the spirit that gives life" (John 6.63). This breath of life comes from the Lord of Creation. However, we must not confuse *man's* spirit with God's Holy Spirit. The latter differs from our human spirit. Romans 8.16 demonstrates their difference by declaring that "it is the Spirit himself bearing witness *with* our spirit that we are children of God." The original of the word "life" in "breath of life" is *chay* and is in the *plural*. This may refer to the fact that the inbreathing of God produced a twofold life, soulical and spiritual. When the inbreathing of God entered man's body it became the spirit of man; but when the spirit reacted with the body the soul was produced. This explains the source of our spiritual and soulical lives. We must recognize, though, that this spirit is not God's *Own* life, for "the breath of the Almighty gives me life" (Job 33.4). It is not the entrance of the uncreated life of God into man, neither is it that life of God which we receive at regeneration. What we receive at new birth is God's Own life as typified by the tree of life. But our human spirit, though permanently existing, is void of "eternal life."

"Formed man of dust from the ground" refers to man's body; "breathed into his nostrils the breath of life" refers to man's spirit as it came from God; and "man became a living soul" refers to man's soul when the body was quickened by the spirit and brought into being a living and self-conscious man. A complete man is a trinity—the composite of spirit, soul and body. According to Genesis 2.7, man was made up of only two independent elements, the corporeal and the spiritual;

but when God placed the spirit within the casing of the earth, the soul was produced. The spirit of man touching the dead body produced the soul. The body apart from the spirit was dead, but with the spirit man was made alive. The organ thus animated was called the soul.

"Man became a living soul" expresses not merely the fact that the combination of spirit and body produced the soul; it also suggests that spirit and body were completely *merged* in this soul. In other words, soul and body were combined with the spirit, and spirit and body were merged in the soul. Adam "in his unfallen state knew nothing of these ceaseless strivings of spirit and flesh which are matters of daily experience to us. There was a perfect *blending* of his three natures into one and the soul as the uniting medium became the cause of his individuality, of his existence as a distinct being." (Pember's *Earth's Earliest Ages*) Man was designated a living soul, for it was there that the spirit and body met and through which his individuality was known. Perhaps we may use an imperfect illustration: drop some dye into a cup of water. The dye and water will blend into a third substance called ink. In like manner the two independent elements of spirit and body combine to become living soul. (The analogy fails in that the soul produced by the combining of spirit and body becomes an independent, indissoluble element as much as the spirit and body.)

God treated man's soul as something unique. As the angels were created as spirits, so man was created predominantly as a living soul. Man not only had a body, a body with the breath of life; he became a living soul as well. Thus we find later in the Scriptures that God often referred to men as "souls." Why? Because what the man is depends on how his soul is. His soul represents him and expresses his individuality. It is the organ of man's free will, the organ in which spirit and body are completely merged. If man's soul wills to obey God, it will allow the spirit to rule over the man as ordered by God. The soul, if it chooses, also can suppress the spirit and take some other delight as lord of the man. This trinity of spirit, soul and body may be partially illustrated by a light bulb. Within the bulb, which can represent the total man, there are electricity, light and wire. The spirit is like the electricity, the soul the light, and body the wire. Electricity is the cause of the light while light is the effect of electricity. Wire is the material substance for carrying the electricity as well as for manifesting the light. The combination of spirit and body produces soul, that which is unique to man. As electricity, carried by the wire, is expressed in light, so spirit acts upon the soul and the soul, in turn, expresses itself through the body.

However, we must remember well that whereas the soul is the meeting-point of the elements of our being in this present life, the spirit will be the ruling power in our resurrection state. For the Bible tells us that "it is sown a physical body, it is raised a spiritual body" (1 Cor. 15.44). Yet here is a vital point: we who have been joined to the resurrected Lord can even now have our spirit rule over the whole being. We are not united to the first Adam who was made a living soul but to the last Adam Who is a life-giving spirit (v.45).

Respective Functions of Spirit, Soul and Body

It is through the corporal body that man comes into contact with the material world. Hence we may label the body as that part which gives us *world-consciousness*. The soul comprises the intellect which aids us in the present state of existence and the emotions which proceed from the senses. Since the soul belongs to man's own self and reveals his personality, it is termed the part of *self-consciousness*. The spirit is that part by which we commune with God and by which alone we are able to apprehend and worship Him. Because it tells us of our relationship with God, the spirit is called the element of *God-consciousness*. God dwells in the spirit, self dwells in the soul, while senses dwell in the body.

As we have mentioned already, the soul is the meeting-point of spirit and body, for there they are merged. By his spirit man holds intercourse with the spiritual world and with the Spirit of God, both receiving and expressing the power and life of the spiritual realm. Through his body man is in contact with the outside sensuous world, affecting it and being affected by it. The soul stands between these two worlds, yet belongs to both. It is linked with the spiritual world through the spirit and with the material world through the body. It also possesses the power of free will, hence is able to choose from among its environments. The spirit cannot act directly upon the body. It needs a medium, and that medium is the soul produced by the touching of the spirit with the body. The soul therefore stands between the spirit and the body, binding these two together. The spirit can subdue the body through the medium of the soul, so that it will obey God; likewise the body through the soul can draw the spirit into loving the world.

Of these three elements the spirit is the noblest for it joins with God. The body is the lowest for it contacts with matter. The soul lying between them joins the two together and also takes their character to be its own. The soul makes it possible for the spirit and the body to communicate and to cooperate. The work of the soul is to keep these two in their proper order so that they may not lose their right relationship—namely, that the lowest, the body, may be subjected to the spirit, and that the highest, the spirit, may govern the body through the soul. Man's prime factor is definitely the soul. It looks to the spirit to give what the latter has received from the Holy Spirit in order that the soul, after it has been perfected, may transmit what it has obtained to the body; then the body too may share in the perfection of the Holy Spirit and so become a spiritual body.

The spirit is the noblest part of man and occupies the innermost area of his being. The body is the lowest and takes the outermost place. Between these two dwells the soul, serving as their medium. The body is the outer shelter of the soul, while the soul is the outer sheath of the spirit. The spirit transmits its thought to the soul and the soul exercises the body to obey the spirit's order. This is the meaning of the soul as the medium. Before the fall of man the spirit controlled the whole being through the soul.

The power of the soul is most substantial, since the spirit and the body are merged there and make it the site of man's personality and influence. Before man committed sin the power of the soul was completely under the dominion of the spirit. Its strength was therefore the spirit's strength. The spirit cannot itself act upon the body; it can only do so through the medium of the soul. This we can see in Luke 1.46-47: "My soul magnifies the Lord, and my spirit has rejoiced in God my Savior" (Darby). "Here the change in tense shows that the spirit first conceived joy in God, and then, communicating with the soul, caused it to give expression to the feeling by means of the bodily organ." (Pember's *Earth's Earliest Ages*)

To repeat, the soul is the site of personality. The will, intellect and emotions of man are there. As the spirit is used to communicate with the spiritual world and the body with the natural world, so the soul stands between and exercises its power to discern and decide whether the spiritual or the natural world should reign. Sometimes too the soul itself takes control over man through its intellect, thus creating an ideational world which reigns. In order for the spirit to govern, the soul must give its consent; otherwise the spirit is helpless to regulate the soul and the body. But this decision is up to the soul, for therein resides the personality of the man.

Actually the soul is the pivot of the entire being, because man's volition belongs to it. It is only when the soul is willing to assume a humble position that the spirit can ever manage the whole man. If the soul rebels against taking such a position the spirit will be powerless to rule. This explains the meaning of the free will of man. Man is not an automaton that turns according to God's will. Rather, man has full sovereign power to decide for himself. He possesses the organ of his own volition and can choose either to follow God's will or to resist Him and follow Satan's will instead. God desires that the spirit, being the noblest part of man, should control the whole being. Yet, the will—the crucial part of individuality—belongs to the soul. It is the will which determines whether the spirit, the body, or even itself is to rule. In view of the fact that the soul possesses such power and is the organ of man's individuality, the Bible calls man "a living soul."

The Holy Temple and Man

"Do you not know," writes the Apostle Paul, "that you are God's temple and that God's Spirit dwells in you?" (1 Cor. 3.16) He has received revelation in likening man to the temple. As God formerly dwelt in the temple, so the Holy Spirit indwells man today. By comparing him to the temple we can see how the tripartite elements of man are distinctly manifested.

We know the temple is divided into three parts. The first is the outer court which is seen by all and visited by all. All external worship is offered here. Going further in is the Holy Place, into which only the priests can enter and where they present oil, incense and bread to God. They are quite near to God—yet not the nearest, for they are still outside the veil and therefore unable to stand before His very presence. God dwells deepest within, in the Holy of Holies, where darkness is overshadowed by brilliant light and into which no man can enter. Though the high priest does enter in once annually, it nonetheless indicates that before the veil is rent there can be no man in the Holy of Holies.

Man is God's temple also, and he too has three parts. The body is like the outer court, occupying an external position with its life visible to all. Here man ought to obey every commandment of God. Here God's Son serves as a substitute and dies for mankind. Inside is man's soul which constitutes the inner life of man and which embraces man's emotion, volition and mind. Such is the Holy Place of a regenerated person, for his love, will and thought are fully enlightened that he may serve God even as the priest of old did. Innermost, behind the veil, lies the Holy of Holies into which no human light has ever penetrated and no naked eye has ever pierced. It is "the secret place of the Most High," the dwelling place of God. It cannot be reached by man unless God is willing to rend the veil. It is man's spirit. This spirit lies beyond man's self-consciousness and above his sensibility. Here man unites and communes with God.

No light is provided for the Holy of Holies because God dwells there. There is light in the Holy Place supplied by the lampstand of seven branches. The outer court stands under the broad daylight. All these serve as images and shadows to a regenerated person. His spirit is like the Holy of Holies indwelt by God, where everything is carried on by faith, beyond the sight, sense or understanding of the believing one. The soul resembles the Holy Place for it is amply enlightened with many rational thoughts and precepts, much knowledge and understanding concerning the things in the ideational and material world. The body is comparable to the outer court, clearly visible to all. The body's actions may be seen by everyone.

The order which God presents to us is unmistakable: "your spirit and soul and body" (1 Thess. 5.23). It is not "soul and spirit and body," nor is it "body and soul and spirit." The spirit is the pre-eminent part, hence it is mentioned first; the body is the lowest and therefore is last mentioned; the soul stands between, so is mentioned between. Having now seen God's order, we can appreciate the wisdom of the Bible in likening man to a temple. We can recognize the perfect harmony which exists between the temple and man in respect to both order and value.

Temple service moves according to the revelation in the Holy of Holies. All activities in the Holy Place and in the outer court are regulated by the presence of God in the Holiest Place. This is the most sacred spot, the place upon which the four corners of the temple converge and rest. It may seem to us that nothing is done in the Holiest because it is pitch dark. All activities are in the Holy Place; even those activities of the outer court are controlled by the priests of the Holy Place. Yet all the activities of the Holy Place actually are directed by the revelation in the utter quietness and peace of the Holy of Holies.

It is not difficult to perceive the spiritual application. The soul, the organ of our personality, is composed of mind, volition and emotion. It appears as though the soul is master of all actions, for the body follows its direction. Before the fall of man, however, the soul, in spite of its many activities, was governed by the spirit. And this is the order God still wants: first the spirit, then the soul, and lastly the body.

A Spiritual Man[12]

A person whose spirit is regenerated and within whom the Holy Spirit abides can still be fleshly for his spirit may yet be under the oppression of his soul or body. Some very definite actions are required if he is to become spiritual.

---

[12] Watchman Nee, *The Spiritual Man*, Vol. II, Part 4, Ch. 2, pp. 18-34.

Generally speaking we will encounter at least two great perils in our life but are enabled to overcome not only the first but the second of them as well. These two perils with their corresponding triumphs are: that of remaining a perishing sinner or becoming a saved believer and that of continuing as a fleshly believer or developing into a spiritual one. As sinner-turned-believer is demonstrably realizable, so carnal-turned-spiritual is likewise attainable. The God Who can change a sinner into a Christian by giving him His life can equally transform the fleshly Christian into a spiritual one by giving him His life more abundantly. Faith in Christ makes one a regenerated believer; obedience to the Holy Spirit makes him a spiritual believer. Just as the right relationship with Christ generates a Christian, so the proper relationship with the Holy Spirit breeds a spiritual man.

The Spirit alone can render believers spiritual. It is His work to bring men into spirituality. In the arrangement of God's redemptive design the cross performs the negative work of destroying all which comes from Adam while the Holy Spirit executes the positive work of building all which comes from Christ. The cross makes spirituality possible to believers; but it is the Holy Spirit Who renders them spiritual. The meaning of being spiritual is to belong to the Holy Spirit. He strengthens with might the human spirit so as to govern the entire man. In our pursuit of spirituality, therefore, we must never forget the Holy Spirit. Yet we must not set aside the cross either, because the cross and the Spirit work hand in hand. The cross always guides men to the Holy Spirit, while the Latter without fail conducts men to the cross. These two never operate independently of each other. A spiritual Christian must experimentally know the Holy Spirit in his spirit. He must pass through several spiritual experiences. For the sake of clarity we shall discuss them in a somewhat sequential fashion, although in actual practice they frequently occur simultaneously.

Quite a few remarks will be made concerning how to be spiritual, but let us not forget what we have learned heretofore. We should realize by now that what hinders one from being spiritual is the flesh. So if a person maintains a proper attitude towards it he shall encounter no difficulty in making progress. It is surprisingly true that the more spiritual one becomes the more he knows the flesh, because he increasingly discovers it. Had he not known it, how could he be spiritual? Hence we cannot neglect what has been discussed earlier concerning the flesh, since it serves as the basis for seeking spirituality. Unless there is this fundamental dealing with the flesh, whatever progress one may make shall inevitably be superficial, shallow, and unreal. But if one knows how to resist his flesh in all things—denying its activity, power, and opinion—he may be regarded as already spiritual. Nevertheless we would still like to cite some positive measures which are related directly to the spirit.

The Dividing of Spirit and Soul

The salient implication of Hebrews 4.12 is whether we are living by intuitive guidance in the spirit or by the naturally good or bad influence of the soul. The Word of God must judge in this particular respect, for only God's sharp Sword can differentiate the source of our living. As a man's knife cuts and divides joints and marrow, so God's Sword too pierces and separates the most intimately linked spirit and soul. Initially such dividing may be simply a matter of knowledge, but it is essential that it enter the realm of experience; otherwise it shall in fact never be understood. Believers should allow the Lord to introduce this cleaving of spirit and soul into their practical walk. Not only must they seek it positively with consecration, prayer, and yieldedness to the operation of the Holy Spirit and the cross, but also they must actually possess such experience. Their spirit needs to be liberated from the soul's binding enclosure. These two must be parted cleanly even as the spirit and soul of the Lord Jesus were not one bit mixed. The intuitive spirit needs to be freed wholly from any influence which may come from soulical mind and emotion. The spirit must be the sole residence and office of the Holy Spirit. It must be released from every disturbance of the soul.

The various experiences of having his outer and inner man divided will make a believer spiritual. A spiritual believer differs from others for the simple reason that his entire being is governed by his spirit.

Such spirit-control connotes more than the Holy Spirit's authority over the soul and body of man; it also signifies that man's *own* spirit, upon being elevated as head over the whole man through the working of the Holy Spirit and the cross, is no longer ruled by the soul and body but is powerful enough to subject them to its rule.

The division of these two organs is necessary for entering spiritual life. It is that preparation without which believers shall continue to be affected by the soul and hence shall always pursue a mixed course: sometimes walking according to the spirit life but at other times walking according to the natural life. Their pathway fails to be marked by purity, for both spirit *and* soul are their life principles. This mixture holds believers fast within a soulish framework which damages their walk as well as hinders the important work of the Spirit.

Were a believer's outer and inner life definitely separated so that he walks not according to the former but according to the latter, he would sense instantaneously any movement in his soul and immediately shake off its power and influence as though being defiled. Indeed, everything belonging to the soulish is defiled and can defile the spirit. But upon experiencing the partition of soul and spirit, the latter's intuitive power becomes most keen. As soon as the soul stirs, the spirit suffers and will resist right away. The spirit may even be grieved at the inordinate stirring of the soul in others. It will in fact repulse a person's soulish love or natural affection as something unbearable. Only after experiencing such separation do Christians come into possession of a genuine sense of cleanliness. They then know that not sin alone, but all which belongs to the soulish, is defiled and defiling and ought to be resisted. Nay, it is far more than simply knowing, for any contact with what is soulish—whether in themselves or in others—causes their intuitive spirit to feel defiled and to demand instant cleansing.

United to the Lord in One Spirit

In his first Corinthian letter, Paul informed his readers that whoever "is united to the Lord becomes one spirit with him" (6.17). And note that he did not say, "one soul with him." The risen Lord is the life-giving Spirit (15.45). His union with the believer is therefore a union with the believer's spirit. The soul, the seat of man's personality, belongs to the natural. All it can and is to be is a vessel for expressing the fruit of the union between the Lord and the believer's inner man. Nothing in his soul partakes of the Lord's life; it is solely in the spirit that such a union is effected. The union is one of spirits with no place for the natural. Should it be mixed in with the spirit it will cause impurity to the union of spirits. Any action taken according to our thought, opinion or feeling can weaken the experimental side of this union. Things of the same nature unite perfectly. Inasmuch as the spirit of the Lord is pure, ours likewise needs to be as pure in order to be united truly with Him. If a believer clings to his own wonderful ideas and is unwilling to lay aside his preference and opinion, his union with the Lord will not be expressed in experience. The union of spirits permits no adulteration from anything soulish.

Wherein lies this union? It is in identification with Christ in His death and resurrection. "If we have been united with him in a death like his, we shall certainly be united with him in a resurrection like his" (Rom. 6.5). This verse explains our union with the Lord as one of being united with His death and resurrection. This simply indicates we are completely one with Him. By accepting His death as our death we enter into this union with the Lord. By additionally accepting His resurrection we who have died with Him shall be resurrected as well. Through faith's acceptance of His resurrection we shall stand experientially in the place of resurrection. Because the Lord Jesus was raised from the dead according to the Spirit of holiness (Rom. 1.4) and was made alive in the spirit (1 Peter 3.18), we too, when united with Him in resurrection, actually are united with Him in His resurrected Spirit. Henceforth we are dead to everything pertaining to ourselves and alive to His Spirit alone. This requires our exercising faith. Once identified with His death, we lose the sinful and the natural in us; once identified with His resurrection, we are united with His resurrection life. Thus our inner being which is now united with the Lord becomes one spirit with Him. "You have died . . . through the body of Christ, so that you may belong to another, to him who has been raised from the dead . . ., so that we serve . . . in the new life of the Spirit" (Rom. 7.4,6). Through Christ's death we are joined to Christ, even in His resurrected life. Such union enables us to serve in the new life of the Spirit, free from any adulteration.

How marvelous is the cross! It is the foundation for everything spiritual. The purpose and end of its working is to unite the believer's spirit with the resurrected Lord into one spirit. The cross must go deeply to rid him of the sinful and the natural within him that he may be joined to the positive resurrection life of the Lord and thus become one spirit with Him. A believer's spirit, together with all which is natural and transient in him, needs to pass through death so that it may be purified and then united to become one spirit with the Lord in the freshness and purity of resurrection. Spirit is joined with Spirit to become one spirit. And the outcome will be: to serve the Lord in "newness of spirit" (Rom. 7.6 Darby). What is of the natural, of self, and of animal activities has no more place in the believer's walk and labor. Both the soul and the body may then but exhibit the purpose, work, and life of the Lord. The Spirit life leaves its imprint on everything, and everything speaks of the out-flowing of the Spirit of the Lord.

This is ascension life. The believer is joined to the Lord Who sits at the right hand of God. The Spirit of the enthroned Lord flows into the spirit of the believer, who is on the earth yet not of the world; the enthroned life is accordingly lived out upon the earth. The Head and the body share the same life. With such a union He is able to pour forth the power of His life through the believer's spirit. As a tube which is connected to a fountain is able to convey living water, so too the believer's spirit which is united with the Spirit of the Lord is capable of transmitting life. The Lord is not just the Spirit; He is the *life-giving* Spirit as well. When our spirit is joined intimately with the life-giving Spirit, it is filled with life; and nothing can limit that life. How we need to have this in our spirit that we may triumph continually in our daily walk. Such a union clothes us with the victory of the Lord Jesus. It gives us the knowledge of His will and mind. It builds and expands the new creation within us by the rich inflow of the Lord's vitality and nature. Through death and resurrection our spirit ascends—even as the Lord has ascended on high—and experiences "the heavenly places," having trodden all that is earthly underfoot. Our inner being is in ascendancy, far above any obstacle or disturbance. Yes, it is continually free and fresh and discerns everything with the transparent sight of heaven. How radically different this life of heaven on earth is from one that is swayed by emotion. The former kind displays heavenly nature and is persistently spiritual.

Knowing the Indwelling of the Holy Spirit

God's children already have the Holy Spirit abiding in them, but they may not recognize Him or obey Him. They need to do so completely. They must realize that this indwelling presence is a Person, One Who teaches, guides, and communicates the reality of Christ to them. Until they are willing to acknowledge the foolishness and dullness of their soul and are ready to be taught, they block the way of this Person. It is necessary for them to let Him regulate everything so as to reveal the truth. Except they know in the depth of their being that God's Holy Spirit is indwelling them and unless with their spirit they wait for His teaching, they will not welcome His operation upon their soul life. Only as they cease to seek anything by themselves and only as they take the position of the teachable shall they be taught by the Spirit truth which they are able to digest. We know He verily abides in us when we understand that our spirit, which is deeper than thought and emotion, is God's Holy of Holies by which we commune with the Holy Spirit and in which we wait for His communication. As we acknowledge Him and respect Him, He manifests His power out from the hidden part of our being by extending His life to our soulical and conscious life.

The Christians at Corinth were of the flesh. In exhorting them to depart from their carnal state, Paul repeatedly reminded them of the fact that they were God's temple and that the Holy Spirit lived in them. Knowing He indwells them helps Christians to overcome their carnal condition. They must know and understand perfectly by faith that He abides in them. Christians should not be content merely with knowing mentally the doctrine of the Holy Spirit as given in the Bible; they also need to know Him experimentally. They will then commit themselves without reservation to Him for renewal and submit every part of their soul and body to His correction.

The Apostle put to those at Corinth this question: "Do you not know that God's Spirit dwells in you?" (1 Cor. 3.16) Paul seemed to be surprised at their ignorance of such a sure fact. He viewed the indwelling of the Holy Spirit as the foremost consequence of salvation, so how could they miss it? However low a Christian's spiritual measure may be, even as low as that of those Christians at Corinth (alas, many probably do not rise higher than that), he nevertheless ought to be clear on this fact without which he shall long remain carnal and never become spiritual. Even if you have not yet *experienced* His indwelling, could you not at least believe he *does* abide in you?

Can we refrain from worship, respect, and praise when we consider how the Holy Spirit—Who is God himself, One of the three Persons in the Triune God, the very life of the Father and the Son—comes to live in us who belong to the flesh? What grace for the Holy Spirit to dwell in the likeness of sinful flesh just as the Lord Jesus once took upon himself the same likeness!

The Strengthening of the Holy Spirit

In order for man's innermost organ to gain dominion over the soul and the body and thus serve as channel for the life of the Spirit to be transmitted to others, there must be His strengthening. Paul prays for believers "that according to the riches of his glory he may grant you to be strengthened with might through his Spirit in the inner man" (Eph. 3.16). He so prays because he considers it infinitely important. He asks God to strengthen by His Spirit their "inner man," which is the new man in them after they have trusted in the Lord. Therefore the prayer is that the believer's spirit may be strengthened by God's Spirit.

From this we may deduce that the spirits of some saints are weak while those of others are strong. Whether they are potent or impotent depends upon whether or not they have received His strengthening. Since those at Ephesus had been sealed already with the Holy Spirit (1.13-14), the Apostle's prayer for them must be concerned with a gift other than His indwelling. His prayer indicates they must have not only the Holy Spirit indwelling them but also have His special power inundating their spirit so as to render their inner man strong. It is possible for us to possess a weak spirit although having God indwelling us.

To be filled with might in the inner man is the urgent need of Christians. However, unless they appreciate how feeble theirs is they will not ask for the invigoration of the Holy Spirit. Often the children of God cannot rise up to answer the Lord's call to service simply because, though their physical condition is good, their feelings are low, cold, and reluctant. Or even when their emotions are quite high, passionate, and willing, they find themselves unable to serve the Lord because now the body reacts lazily. Such phenomena betray the weakness of the spirit in its dominion over feeling and the physical body. The disciples found themselves in precisely that situation in the Garden of Gethsemane: "the spirit indeed is willing, but the flesh is weak" (Matt. 26.41). Willingness by itself is not sufficient; the spirit also must be strong. If it is sturdy it can overcome the infirmity of the flesh. Why do believers sometimes find themselves dragging and failing while laboring for souls? Lack of power in their spirit is the explanation. The same holds true in the case of environment. How easily we are affected by the confusion of the outside world. Were our spirits hardy we would be able to meet the most disturbing situation with peace and rest. Prayer is the acid test of the inner man's strength. A strong spirit is capable of praying much and praying with all perseverance until the answer comes. A weak one grows weary and fainthearted in the maintenance of praying. A vigorous spirit can move forward in the midst of adverse environment or feeling, but a frail one is impotent to stand against opposition. Great is the need of power in the spirit for spiritual warfare with Satan. Only those who have might in the inner man understand how to exercise their spiritual strength in resisting and attacking the enemy. Otherwise the battle will be make-believe, fought in the imagination of the mind or the excitement of the emotion, and perhaps fought with the weapons of flesh and blood.

In order for the inner man to be strengthened with power through the Holy Spirit, the children of God must discharge their responsibility. They need to yield specifically to the Lord, forsake every doubtful aspect in their life, be willing to obey fully God's will, and believe through prayer that He will flood their spirit with His power. Without delay God will answer the expectation of their heart, once all obstacles on their part are removed. Believers do not need to wait for the Holy Spirit's filling, because He has descended already. What they need only wait for is for themselves to fulfill the condition for His filling, which is, they must let the cross perform a deeper incision upon them. Should they be faithful in believing and obeying, then within a very short time the power of the Holy Spirit will saturate their spirit and strengthen their inner man for living and for laboring. Some may receive His filling immediately upon once surrendering themselves to the Lord, for they already have met the conditions for such filling.

This invasion of God's power in us, this infilling of His Spirit, happens in the human spirit. It is the inner and not the outer man which is activated by His power and thence becomes strong. This is most important to recognize, for it helps us to exercise simple faith in our desire for the filling of the Holy Spirit (Gal. 3.14), rather than to anticipate some bodily sensations such as a shaking, a jerking, or a hurling to the ground. Yet Christians need to be watchful lest they use faith as an excuse for not experiencing the empowering of the Holy

Spirit. The conditions for filling must be accomplished and the attitude of believers must be firm. God will fulfill His promise.

By reading what the Apostle affirms in the succeeding verses in Ephesians 3 about apprehending, knowing, and filling, we are certain this strengthening with might in the inner man renders it highly sensitive. Like the body, the spirit has its functions and consciousness. Prior to the mighty inflow of the Holy Spirit's power into their spirit, believers scarcely can detect its intuitive power; but afterwards its intuitive force becomes most distinctive and hence readily discovered. As the inner man is energized, its intuitive power is increased. Believers are able to sense its slightest movement.

The effect of having the spirit filled with God's power is to afford it full sway over the soul and the body. Every thought, desire, sensation and intent is now governed by the spirit. The soul can no longer act independently: it becomes instead the spirit's steward. Furthermore, through the believer's spirit the Holy Spirit is able to impart God's life to thirsty and dying men. However, this filling of the Holy Spirit differs from the so called baptism with the Holy Spirit, because the latter is for the purpose of service while the former solves the problem of life (naturally it will affect service too).

Walking According to the Spirit

Transformation from soulish to spiritual does not guarantee that believers never again will walk according to the flesh. On the contrary, an ever present danger exists of falling back into it. Satan is constantly alert to seize every opportunity to cause them to plunge from their lofty position to a life below par. It is therefore highly necessary for God's children to be watchful at all times and to follow the Spirit so that they may remain spiritual.

"In order that the just requirement of the law might be fulfilled in us, who walk not according to the flesh but according to the Spirit . . . (Now) those who live according to the Spirit set their minds on the things of the Spirit. To set . . . the mind on the Spirit is life and peace" (Rom. 8.4-6). To follow the spirit is to walk contrary to the flesh. Not following the spirit is walking by the flesh. Many Christians oscillate between these two: now following the one, now following the other. They ought to walk according to the inner man *alone*, which is, to walk according to the spirit's intuition and not for a moment according to the soul or body. In thus following the spirit they invariably shall "set their minds on the things of the spirit." And the result shall be "life and peace."

To live by the spirit means to walk according to intuition. It is to have all one's life, service, and action in the spirit, ever being governed and empowered by it.

This preserves the saint in life and peace. Since he cannot remain in a spiritual state unless he walks according to the spirit, then at the very least the saint must understand its various functions and laws if he is to walk well.

To live after the spirit is the Christian's daily task. He ought to perceive that we can live neither by the noblest of feelings nor by the loftiest of thoughts. We must walk according to the guidance accorded us through our intuition. The Holy Spirit expresses His feeling through our spirit's delicate sense. He does not operate directly on our minds, suddenly inducing us to think of something. All His works are done in our innermost depths. If we desire to know His mind we should conduct ourselves in accordance with the intuition of our spirit. At times, however, we may sense something there without comprehending what it means, what it demands, or what it is communicating. Whenever this happens, we must commit ourselves to prayer, asking that our mind may be given understanding. Once we apprehend the meaning of what we have sensed intuitively, we thereafter should behave accordingly. The mind can instantly be enlightened and made to understand the meaning of intuition; but abrupt thoughts which originate with the mind void of intuition ought not to be followed. Solely intuitive teaching represents the Spirit's thought. Only this should we follow.

Such a walk by the spirit requires *reliance* and *faith*. We have seen before how all good actions of the flesh exhibit an attitude of independence towards God. The very nature of the soul is independency. Should believers act in accordance with their thought, feeling and desire, they have no need to spend time before God, to wait for His guidance. Those who follow "the desires of body and mind" (Eph. 2.3) need not rely upon God. Except Christians realize how useless, how undependable, and how utterly weak they are in seeking to know the will of God, they shall never cultivate a heart of reliance upon Him. To receive God's guidance in their spirit they must wait upon Him therewith; they must refrain from taking their feeling or thought as a guide. Let us remember that whatever we do or can do without trusting, seeking, and waiting upon God is or will be done in the flesh. With fear and trembling we must rely upon God for guidance in the inner depths. This is the sole way to walk according to the spirit.

To walk in this fashion requires faith of the believer. The opposite of sight and feeling is faith. Now it is the soulish person who gains assurance by grasping the things which can be seen and felt; but the person who follows the spirit lives by faith, not by sight. He will not be troubled by the lack of human assistance, nor will he be moved by human opposition. He can trust God even in utter darkness for he has faith in God. Because he does not depend upon himself, he can trust the unseen power more than his own visible power.

Walking after the spirit involves both the initiation of a work by revelation and execution of it through the Lord's strength. Frequently believers beseech God for spiritual power to do a work which has not been revealed at all in their intuition. This is simply impossible, for what is of the flesh is flesh. On the other hand believers frequently know the will of God through revelation in their intuition but bring their own strength to the work to perform it. This likewise is impossible, for how can they begin with the Holy Spirit and end up with the flesh? Those who follow the Lord must be brought to the place of no confidence in the flesh. They must confess they can originate no good idea and must admit they possess no power to fulfill the Holy Spirit's work. All thought, cleverness, knowledge, talent and gift—which the world superstitiously worships—must be set aside in order to enable one to trust the Lord wholly. The Lord's people should persistently acknowledge their own unworthiness and incompetency. They dare not initiate anything before receiving God's order nor attempt to execute God's command in self-reliance.

To live by the spirit we must move in accordance with the delicate sense of its intuition and depend on its enabling to accomplish the revealed task. Well do we begin if we follow intuition instead of thought, opinion, feeling or tendency; well do we end if we rely on the Spirit's power and not on our talent, strength or ability. Simply keep in mind that the moment we cease to follow our intuitive sense at that very moment we begin to walk after the flesh and end up minding the things of the flesh. This in turn injects death into the spirit. Only if we "walk not according to the flesh" can we walk "according to the spirit."

Our aim is to be a spiritual man but not a spirit. If we recognize this distinction our lives shall never be cut and dried. We today are human beings and shall be so eternally, yet the highest achievement of a human being is to develop into a spiritual man. The angels are spirits; they have neither body nor soul. But we humans possess both. We are to be spiritual *men* and not spirits. The spiritual man shall continue to retain his soul and body; otherwise, he would be reduced to being a spirit instead of a man. No, what is meant by being a spiritual man is that he is under the control of his spirit which has become the highest organ of his whole person. Let us not be mistaken on this point. A spiritual man retains his soul and body; being spiritual does not annihilate these organs nor their respective functions, because these make man what he is. So although the spiritual man does not live by them, he certainly has not annihilated them either. They instead have been renewed through death and resurrection so that they are perfectly united to the spirit and have become instruments for its expression. Hence the emotion, mind and will remain in a spiritual man but are subject entirely to the guidance of the intuition.

The emotion of a spiritual man is completely under his spirit's regulation, no longer asserting an independent course as it once did. It does not block the spirit nor resist its move because it does not insist upon its own affection and feeling. The emotion now rejoices solely in what the spirit likes, loves only what the spirit directs, feels merely what the spirit permits. It has become its life: when the spirit stirs, emotion responds.

The mind of the spiritual man likewise cooperates with the spirit, wandering no more as in the past. It does not object to the spirit's revelation by raising its reason and argument, neither does it disturb the peace of the spirit with many confused thoughts, nor does it rebel against the spirit by boasting in its own wisdom. Quite the reverse, the mind cooperates fully with the intuition in advancing on the spiritual journey. If the spirit unfolds any revelation the mind discerns its meaning. It will assist the spirit to fight should the latter plunge into warfare. If the Holy Spirit desires to teach any truth, the mind will help the spirit to understand. The latter, though, has the authority to stop the mind's thinking as well as to initiate it.

The spiritual man also retains his will, yet it too is no longer independent of God but now decides according to the dictate of the spirit, having abandoned self as its center. The will does not insist upon its desire as before. It consequently is fit to obey God. No more is it hard and stiff but is completely broken; hence it cannot resist God or strive against Him. It has been tamed of its wild nature. Today when the spirit receives revelation and apprehends God's wish, the will decides to follow. It stands at the spirit's door like a courier, awaiting its every command.

The body of a spiritual man is subjected to the spirit as well. Because it has been cleansed by the precious blood and has had its passions and lusts dealt with by the cross, it can serve today as an obedient servant to the spirit's order as that order is communicated to the body from the spirit through the soul. By no means does it entice the soul into many sins by its passions and lusts as it formerly did. Instead the body now answers swiftly all the spirit's directions. The latter through the renewed will has complete authority over the body. Gone are the days when the body pressed a weak inner man. The spirit of a spiritual man has grown strong and the body is under its power.

The Apostle Paul has described the authentic condition of a spiritual man in 1 Thessalonians: "May the God of peace himself sanctify you wholly; and may your spirit and soul and body be kept sound and blameless at the coming of our Lord Jesus Christ" (5.23). Hence the portrait of the spiritual man which can be drawn from everything which has been said is as follows:

(1) He has God dwelling in his spirit, sanctifying him totally. Its life inundates his entire person so that his every component lives by the spirit life and functions in the spirit's strength.

(2) He does not live by soul life. His every thought, imagination, feeling, idea, affection, desire and opinion is renewed and purified by the Spirit and has been brought

into subjection to his spirit. These no longer operate independently.

(3) He still possesses a body, for he is not a disembodied spirit; yet physical weariness, pain, and demand do not impel the spirit to topple from its ascended position. Every member of the body has become an instrument of righteousness.

To conclude, then, a spiritual man is one who belongs to the spirit: the whole man is governed by the inner man: all the organs of his being are subject completely to it. His spirit is what stamps his life as unique—everything proceeds from his spirit, while he himself renders absolute allegiance to it. No word does he speak nor act does he perform according to himself; rather does he deny his natural power each time in order to draw power from the spirit. In a word, a spiritual man lives by the spirit.

The Second Stage of My Spiritual Journey (1928-1942)

From the Expansion of the Work to His Withdrawal from Ministry

In 1928 a gathering of Christians began to meet at Wen Teh Lane, along Hardoon Road, Shanghai. There Watchman Nee experienced deliverance from sin: "The fact that you are in Christ Jesus," he would relate later, "is *God's* doing! It was amazing! So then, if Christ died, and that is a certain fact, and if God put me in Him, then *I* must have died too. All at once I saw my oneness with Christ—that I was in Him and that when He died I died. My death to sin was a matter of the past and not of the future. It was Divine fact that had dawned on me."

It was also there that Watchman Nee experienced the healing of his deadly disease of tuberculosis. He was dying; but, then, the Lord gave him three words from the Scriptures regarding faith: "in faith ye *stand* fast" (II

Corinthians 1:24b), "we *walk* by faith" (II Corinthians 5:7), and "the righteous shall *live* by faith" (Romans 1:17b). He rejoiced and thanked God that his Lord had healed him. He was no longer bedridden.

The work continued to grow and soon assemblies were raised up everywhere along the eastern coast of China. War broke out between China and Japan in 1937. In the middle of 1938 brother Nee revisited England, and ministered both there and in Denmark. In Denmark he delivered a series of messages on Romans chapters 5-8, which he had entitled, "The Normal Christian Life."

Returning to Shanghai in July of 1939, Watchman took upon himself the work of training his fellow workers. Realizing, however, that the war would be long and the financial needs of the work would be great, he went into a business that ultimately proved to be a dark chapter in his life. He was greatly misunderstood by the church-at-large, with the result that at the end of 1942 he was asked by the responsible brothers of the assembly at Shanghai to discontinue ministering there.

When one reads his writings during this period, it is noticeable that Watchman Nee's burden was twofold: the proper spiritual growth of every Christian's life and having a clear understanding of the church of God. For him these two must go together. The Lord seemed to give him greater understanding on Christian life, he speaking on this quite often wherever he traveled. At this same time brother Nee also received a clearer understanding of what a local assembly is, having found and embraced the middle ground between the teaching of the Open Brethren and that of the Exclusive Brethren.

On the one hand, brother Nee took the position of the oneness of the church universal, even as both these two branches of the Brethren stand for; on the other hand, he differed from both branches concerning the teaching and practice of the local church. He espoused the principle of one church one locality, contrary to both the Open Brethren who believed in many churches one locality and the Exclusive Brethren who stood for the control of all the local churches under one authority. A locality is where the aggregate of people are known to one another, and not a modern metropolitan city. These are the two aspects of the church as was revealed to Watchman Nee during this stage in his spiritual journey. What follows are extracts selected from the author's spoken ministry that are reflective of this second stage in his spiritual journey.

1: Excerpts from *The Normal Christian Life*

[13]What is the normal Christian life? We do well at the outset to ponder this question. The object of these studies is to show that it is something very different from the life of the average Christian. Indeed a consideration of the written Word of God—of the Sermon on the Mount for example—should lead us to ask whether such a life has ever in fact been lived upon the earth, *save only by the Son of God himself*. But in that last saving clause lies immediately the answer to our question.

The Apostle Paul gives us his own definition of the Christian life in Galatians 2:20. It is "no longer I, but Christ." Here he is not stating something special or peculiar—a high level of Christianity. He is, we believe, presenting God's normal for a Christian, which can be summarized in the words: I live no longer, but Christ lives His life in me.

God makes it quite clear in His Word that He has only one answer to every human need—His Son, Jesus Christ. In all His dealings with us He works by taking *us*

---

[13] Watchman Nee, *The Normal Christian Life* (Ft. Washington PA: Christian Literature Crusade, 2012), pp. 9-10. The contents of this book is based primarily on the author's spoken ministry in English delivered in Denmark in 1938, was first published at Bombay, India by Gospel Literature Service in 1957, was revised in 1961, and reprinted numerous times ever since.—*Translator*

out of the way and substituting Christ in our place. The Son of God died instead of us for our forgiveness: He lives instead of us for our deliverance. So we can speak of two substitutions—a Substitute on the Cross who secures our forgiveness and a Substitute within who secures our victory. It will help us greatly, and save us from much confusion, if we keep constantly before us this fact, that God will answer all our questions in one way only, namely, by showing us more of His Son.

The Path of Progress

[14]As we study chapters 6, 7 and 8 of Romans we shall discover that the conditions of living the normal Christian life are fourfold. They are: (a) Knowing, (b) Reckoning, (c) Presenting ourselves to God, and (d) Walking in the Spirit, and they are set forth in that order. If we would live that life we shall have to take all four of these steps [in pursuing the path of progress]; not one nor two nor three, but all four.

The First Step: "Knowing This ..."

[15]..."I was crucified when Christ was crucified" or "Christ was crucified when I was crucified," for they are not two historical events, but one. My crucifixion was

[14] Watchman Nee, *The Normal Christian Life*, Ch. 3, pp. 41-42.
[15] *Ibid.*, p. 43.

"[16]with him." Has Christ been crucified? Then can I be otherwise? And if He was crucified nearly two thousand years ago, and I with Him, can my crucifixion be said to take place tomorrow? Can His be past and mine be present or future? Praise the Lord, when He died on the cross, I died with Him. He not only died in my stead, but He bore me with Him to the Cross, so that when He died I also died. And if I believe in the death of the Lord Jesus, then I can believe in my own death just as surely as I believe in His.

The Second Step: "Even So Reckon ..."

[17]What does reckoning mean? "Reckoning" in Greek means doing accounts, bookkeeping. Accounting is the only thing in the world we human beings can do correctly. An artist paints a landscape. Can he do it with perfect accuracy? Can the historian vouch for the absolute accuracy of any record, or the map-maker for the perfect correctness of any map? They can make, at best, fair approximations. Even in everyday speech, when we try to tell some incident with the best intention to be honest and truthful, we cannot speak with complete accuracy. It is mostly a case of exaggeration or understatement, of one word too much or too little.

---

[16] The expression "with him" in Romans 6:6 carries of course a doctrinal as well as historical, or temporal sense. It is only in the historical sense that the statement is reversible.—W.N.

[17] *Ibid.*, Ch. 4, pp. 56-57.

What then can a man do that is utterly reliable? Arithmetic! There is no scope for error there. One chair plus one chair equals two chairs. That is true in London and it is true in Cape Town. If you travel west to New York or east to Singapore it is still the same. All the world over and for all time, one plus one equals two. One plus one is two in heaven and earth and hell.

Why does God say we are to reckon ourselves dead? Because we *are* dead.

The Third Step: "Present Yourselves ..."

[18]Let us observe that this "presenting" relates to the members of my body—that body which, as we said earlier, is now unemployed in respect to sin. "Present yourselves ... and your members," says Paul, and again: "Present your members" (Romans 6:13, 19). God requires of me that I now regard all my members, all my faculties, as belonging wholly to Him.

[19]Presenting myself to God implies a recognition that I am altogether His. This giving of myself is a definite thing, just as definite as reckoning. There must be a day in my life when I pass out of my own hands into His, and from that day forward I belong to Him and no longer to myself.

---

[18] *Ibid.*, Ch. 6, p. 88.
[19] *Ibid.*, p. 90.

The Fourth Step: "Walk ... after the Spirit"

[20]What does it mean to walk after the Spirit? It means two things. Firstly, it is not a work; it is a walk. Praise God, the burdensome and fruitless effort I involved myself in when I sought "in the flesh" to please God gives place to a blessed and restful dependence on "his working, which worketh in me mightily" (Col. 1:29). That is why Paul contrasts the "works" of the flesh with the "fruit" of the Spirit (Gal. 5:19, 22).

Then secondly, to "walk after" implies subjection. Walking after the flesh means that I yield to the dictates of the flesh, and the following verses in Romans 8:5-8 make clear where that leads me. It only brings me into conflict with God. To walk after the Spirit is to be subject to the Spirit. There is one thing that the man who walks after the Spirit cannot do, and that is be independent of Him. I *must* be subject to the Holy Spirit. The initiative of my life must be with Him. Only as I yield myself to obey Him shall I find the "law of the Spirit of life" in full operation and the "ordinance of the law" (all that I have been trying to do to please God) being fulfilled—no longer *by* me but *in* me. "As many as are led by the Spirit of God, these are sons of God" (Rom. 8:14).

---

[20] *Ibid.*, Ch. 10, p. 175.

CHRIST OUR LIFE[21]

"I thank God through Jesus Christ"! That exclamation of Paul's is fundamentally the same in its import as his other words in Galatians 2:20 which we have taken as the key to our study: "I live; and yet no longer I, *but Christ*." We saw how prominent is the word "I" throughout Romans 7, culminating in the agonized cry, "O wretched man that I am!" Then follows the shout of deliverance: "Thank God ... *Jesus Christ*"! and it is clear that the discovery Paul has made is this, that *the life we live is the life of Christ alone*. We think of the Christian life as a "changed life," but it is not that. What God offers us is an "exchanged life," a "substituted life," and Christ is our Substitute within. "I live; and yet no longer I, but Christ liveth in me." This life is not something which we ourselves have to produce. It is Christ's own life reproduced in us.

How many Christians believe in "reproduction" in this sense, as something more than regeneration? Regeneration means that the life of Christ is planted in us by the Holy Spirit at our new birth. "Reproduction" goes further: it means that new life grows and becomes manifest progressively in us, until the very likeness of Christ begins to be reproduced in our lives. That is what Paul means when he speaks of his travail for the Galatians "until Christ be formed in you" (Gal. 4:19).

---

[21] *Ibid.*, p. 160.

2: EXCERPTS FROM *THE CHURCH AND THE WORK*

THE CHURCH IS ONE[22]

The Bible teaches that the Church is one. The Church which Paul belonged to is the same Church to which we all belong. Our Church is the Church also of the apostle John, Martin Luther, Calvin and all the other regenerated people throughout Church history. The Church of the Bible has no distinction as to time, geography, or race. In the eyes of God, from the beginning to the end, past and present, at home and abroad, there is only one Church, not two or more Churches. The Bible recognizes the body of Christ, which is one and one only. There can never be two bodies of Christ because there is but one Head. Though the members are many, the body is one. Hence all the saved people, ancient and modern, at home and abroad, form one Church, one body.

Why, then, are there "the churches" in various places? Since the Letter to the Ephesians speaks of one

---

[22] Watchman Nee, *The Church and the Work*, 3 Vols, translated from the Chinese (New York: Christian Fellowship Publishers, 1982), Vol. I (*Assembly Life*), Ch. 2, pp. 49-51. The contents of this trilogy's first volume consist of notes of a series of Bible studies the author had conducted at Shanghai during late February 1934. These notes were subsequently published in Chinese.—*Translator*

body, one Spirit, one hope, one Lord, one faith, one baptism and one God (Eph. 4.4-6), why do the Scriptures mention the churches? Is there any contradiction in the Bible? For it speaks of one body on the one hand and the churches on the other. This tells us of the different aspects of the Church. Actually, there is only one Church, for the body of Christ is one. But in different localities, there may be as many as three to five thousand believers gathered together or as little as two or three (Matt. 18.20). In any city or village where a group of believers is gathered together, those believers there are the church in that city or village. The Scriptures most emphatically employ the phrase "the church in (or at)" such and such a place. The word "in" shows us that the Church is one, even though its various members are scattered and sojourn in many, many localities. The Bible treats all the believers who sojourn in a given locality as constituting the local church, a miniature representative of the one and only Church.

One thing is exceedingly precious: "We, who are many, are one bread" (1 Cor. 10.17). The "we" here includes all the believers. There is only one loaf. Hence do not imagine that there is one loaf in Shanghai and another loaf in Peking, and so forth. From the physical viewpoint, there may be tens of thousands of loaves throughout the world; from the spiritual viewpoint, however, there is but one bread loaf before God. Why is there but one loaf? Because being in the flesh we are restricted by time and space. If it were possible, all the believers in the entire world would break one loaf of bread together. But we know that that is not possible. Even so, though all the believers in all the different places throughout the world break the bread respectively, before God there is but one bread loaf being broken. The bread which the hands of the brethren in Shanghai touch is the same bread which the brethren in Peking and the brethren in Hanchow touch. The bread which is broken everywhere represents the one body of Christ. For God has only one Church in the world. And this Church is spread out throughout every city and every village world-wide. And the churches which are thus spread out are called the churches in these cities and villages. For the sake of convenience, these churches in the many cities and villages of the world are called "the churches of God" (2 Thess. 1.4; 1 Cor. 11.16; cf. also 1 Thess. 2.14). In actuality, the churches of God are the Church of God. The Lord calls us to break bread lest we forget the churches at various places. We are not to be an independent church, but to be joined with others as one Church. This is why we use one bread loaf to aid us in recognizing that though there are many believers—past and present, at home and abroad—and many local churches, there is nevertheless but one loaf of bread.

The bread which we believers world-wide break may amount to tens of thousands of loaves, yet the body of Christ which the bread represents is only one. The Lord that the bread speaks of is also one. So that all the miniature local churches stand for the entire body of Christ. A local assembly may have only fifty people gathered together, but what it represents is the entire body of believers, both past and present, at home and abroad. The bread which any local assembly breaks, however small that assembly may be, represents Peter, Paul, Martin Luther, Wesley, and you and me. Wherever the local assembly is, it is a representation of the body of Christ. Therefore no church may take independent action. In all its actions it must take the entire body into consideration. In the meeting, you should not see just the few brothers and sisters who sit by you; instead you should see the entire body of Christ. What you do is not only related to the brothers and sisters immediately around you but it is also related to the whole body of Christ. Because we are one body, what you as a member do is what the body of Christ does. One member may affect the whole body.

The Border of a Local Assembly[23]

Concerning the border of a local assembly, in the New Testament God makes the city to be its boundary. So that the maximum sphere of a local assembly is a city and nothing larger than a city. In the biblical record, there is no church that controls a region, a province, or a county. The city always marks the limit of the church. A

---

[23] *Ibid.*, Ch. 4, p. 102.

city was originally the aggregate of people who lived in the same locality. Let us realize that due to today's complicated life we have such divisions as county, township, village, and so forth. In the olden days, wherever the people congregated and lived and were protected—that was considered a city (Gen. 4.17). For various reasons, they lived in the city. In the first part of Genesis we find nothing smaller than the city. At the time when Joshua apportioned the land to the Hebrew people, we notice that the place where people lived was still called a city, only now sometimes villages were also mentioned (see Joshua 18.28). When the Lord Jesus sent out His disciples to preach the gospel, they were sent to cities (see Matt. 10). This is because in the biblical account a city was viewed as the lowest unit of the aggregate of people.

Thus the boundary of a local assembly in the Scriptures is according to the limit of such a city. Ephesus, Corinth, and Thessalonica, for example, were all such cities. The border of a local church never exceeds the limit of a city. The province of Asia was such a large area that it had seven churches. Galatia was a region, and hence the phrase "the churches in Galatia" was used. Corinth, on the other hand, was only a city, and so the whole church assembled together there (1 Cor. 14.23). The church in Corinth is but one church. Throughout the New Testament we see that all the local assemblies take the particular city limits as their border.

[24]Questions will naturally arise concerning large cities such as London. Do they reckon one "unit-locality," or more than one? London is clearly not a "city" in the scriptural sense of the term, and it cannot therefore be regarded as a unit. Even people living in London talk about going "into the city," or "into town," which reveals the fact that, in their thinking, "London" and "the city" are not synonymous. The political and postal authorities, as well as the man on the street, regard London as more than one unit. They divide it respectively into boroughs and postal districts. What they regard as an administrative unit, we may well regard as a church unit.

As to country-places which could not technically be termed "cities," they may also be regarded as "unit-localities." It is said of our Lord, when on earth, that He went out into the "cities and villages" (Luke 13.22), from which we see that country-places, as well as towns, are considered to be separate units.

[25]It is death to have a wine-skin without wine, but it is loss to have wine without a wine-skin. We must have the wine-skin *after* we have the wine. Paul wrote the

---

[24] *Ibid.*, Vol. II (*Rethinking the Work*), Ch. 5, pp. 90-91. This trilogy's second volume consists of the text of the talks which the author delivered at two separate conferences which he had convened at Shanghai and Hankow in 1937. These talks were collected and published in Chinese at Shanghai in January 1938 under the title, *Rethinking the Work.*

[25] *Ibid.*, Vol. II, Introduction, pp. 5-6.

Ephesian Epistle, but he could also write the Corinthian Epistle; and Corinthians presents us with Ephesian truths in practical expression. Yes, the writer of Ephesians was also the writer of Corinthians! But why is it that the children of God have never had any serious contentions over Ephesian truths, but always over Corinthian truths? Because the sphere of Ephesians is the Heavenlies, and its truths are purely spiritual, so if there is any diversity of opinion concerning them, no one feels it much; but Corinthian teachings are practical and touch the earthly sphere, so if there is the slightest difference of opinion a reaction is felt at once. Yes, Corinthians is very practical! And it tests our obedience more than does Ephesians!

The danger, with those who know little about life and reality, is to emphasize mere outward correctness: but with those to whom life and reality are a matter of supreme importance, the temptation is to throw away the Divine pattern of things, thinking it legal and technical. They feel that they have the greater and can therefore well dispense with the lesser. As a result, the more spiritual a man is, the freer he feels to do as he thinks fit. He considers that he himself has authority to decide on outward matters, and rather fancies that to ignore God's commands regarding them is an indication that he has been delivered from legality and is walking in the liberty of the Spirit. But God has not only revealed the truths that concern our inner life. He has also revealed the truths relating to the outward expression of that life. God prizes the inner reality, but He does not ignore its outward expression. God has given us Ephesians, Romans and Colossians, but He has also given us Acts, the Epistles to Timothy and the Epistles to the Corinthians. We might deem it sufficient for God to instruct us through Romans, Ephesians and Colossians as to our life in Christ, but He has deemed it necessary to instruct us through Acts, Corinthians and Timothy, how to do His Work and how to organize His Church. God has left nothing to human imagination or human will. Man is afraid to use a thoughtless servant, but God does not care to use an over-thoughtful one; all He requires of man is simple obedience. "Who hath been his counsellor?" asked Paul (Rom. 11.34). Man would fain occupy the post, but God has no need of a counsellor. It is not our place to suggest how we think Divine Work should be done, but rather to ask in everything, "What is the Will of the Lord?"

[26]Since the meaning of the word "apostle" is "the sent one," the meaning of apostleship is quite plain, i.e. the office of the sent one. Apostles are not primarily men of special gifts, they are men of special commission. Everyone who is sent of God is an apostle. Many called of God are not as gifted as Paul, but if they have received a commission from God, they are just as truly apostles as he was. The apostles were gifted men, but their apostleship was not based upon their gifts; it was based

[26] *Ibid.*, Ch. 2, pp. 41-42.

upon their commission. Of course, God will not send anyone who is unequipped, but equipment does not constitute apostleship. If God cared to send out a man totally unequipped, that man would be as much an apostle as a fully equipped one, since apostleship is not based on human qualification but on Divine commission. It is futile for anyone to assume the office of an apostle simply because he thinks he has the needed gifts or ability. It takes more than mere gift and ability to constitute men apostles; it takes nothing less than God himself, God's Will and God's call. No man can attain to apostleship through natural or other qualifications; God must make him an apostle if he is ever to be one. Whether or not a man is going to be of any spiritual worth, and his work serve any spiritual end, depends upon the sending of God. "A man sent of God" should be the main characteristic of our entering upon His service, and of all our subsequent movements.

Let us turn to the Scriptures. In Luke 11.49 we read: "I will send them prophets and apostles, and some of them they shall slay and persecute." From the Book of Genesis to the Book of Malachi we do not come across anyone who was explicitly called an apostle, yet the men here referred to as apostles lived between the time of Abel and Zecharias (verse 51), so it is clear that even in Old Testament times God had His apostles.

Our Lord said, "The servant is not greater than his Lord: neither the apostle (Greek) than he that sent him" (John 13.16). Here we have a definition of the term "apostle." It implies being sent out—that is all; and that is everything. However good human intention may be, it can never take the place of Divine commission. To-day those who have been sent out by the Lord to preach the Gospel and to establish churches call themselves missionaries, not apostles; but the word "missionary" means the very same thing as "apostle," i.e. "the sent one." It is the Latin form of the Greek equivalent, "apostolos." Since the meaning of the two words is exactly the same, I fail to see the reason why the *true* sent ones of to-day prefer to call themselves "missionaries" rather than "apostles."

[27]Elders were local men appointed to oversee affairs in the local church. Their sphere of office was limited by the locality. An elder in Ephesus was not an elder in Smyrna, and an elder in Smyrna was not an elder in Ephesus. In Scripture there are no local apostles, nor are there any extra-local elders; all elders are local, and all apostles are extra-local. The Word of God nowhere speaks of apostles managing the affairs of a local church, and it nowhere speaks of elders managing the affairs of several local churches. The apostles were the ministers of all the churches, but they had control of none; the elders were confined to one church and they controlled affairs in that one. The duty of apostles was to found churches. Once a church was established, all

[27] *Ibid.*, Ch. 4, pp. 76-78.

responsibility was handed over to the local elders, and from that day the apostles exercised no control whatever in its affairs. All management was in the hands of the elders, and if they thought right they could even refuse an apostle entry into their church. Should such a thing occur, the apostle would have no authority to insist on being received, since all local authority had already passed from his hands into the hands of the elders.

How did Paul deal with the adulterous believer in Corinth? He did not just notify the church that *he* had excommunicated the man. The utmost he could do was to instruct its members regarding the seriousness of the situation and seek to admonish them to remove the wicked person from their midst (1 Cor. 5.13). If the church was right spiritually they would pay attention to Paul, but if they disregarded his exhortations, whilst they would be wrong spiritually, they would not be wrong legally. In the event of their despising his counsel, Paul could only bring his spiritual authority to bear on the situation. In the Name of the Lord Jesus he could "deliver such a one unto Satan for the destruction of the flesh" (verse 5). He had no official authority to discipline him, but he had spiritual authority to deal with the case. He had his spiritual "rod."

The affairs of the local church are entirely independent of the apostles. Once elders have been appointed, all control passes into their hands, and whilst thereafter an apostle may still instruct and persuade, he can never interfere. But this did not hinder Paul from speaking authoritatively to the Corinthians. Even a casual reader will notice how authoritative his statements were in both epistles. It was quite within his province to pass judgment where doctrinal and moral questions were concerned, and when Paul did so he was most emphatic; but the actual enforcing of such judgments was outside his province and entirely a matter for the local church.

An apostle can deal with the disorders of a church whenever his advice and counsel are sought, as was the case with Paul and the church in Corinth. It was because of their enquiries that he could say to them, "And the rest will I set in order whensoever I come" (1 Cor. 11.34). But the point to note here is that "the rest" of the matters which Paul intended to "set in order" on his arrival in Corinth were to be attended to in the same way as those he had dealt with in his Epistle, and they were dealt with *doctrinally*. In like manner as he had instructed them concerning certain affairs there, so he would instruct them concerning the remaining matters on his arrival; but the Corinthians themselves, not Paul, were the ones who would have *to deal* with the situation.

The Third Stage of My Spiritual Journey (1942-1952)

From the Recovery of Ministry to His Captivity

Believing in the sanctity of the church, Watchman accepted the decision of the Shanghai assembly in late 1942 and retreated to the city of Foochow. There he quietly prepared for the future. He began to buy some houses on Kuling Mountain outside Foochow in preparation for establishing a future training ground. Meanwhile he patiently endured all misunderstanding and refused to defend himself. Later he traveled to Chungking, the war capital of Free China. There, at the earnest and persistent requests of the saints who gathered in the name of the Lord Jesus in that capital city and the surrounding suburban areas, he ministered God's word to them for a short period. It was here that he delivered the messages on "The Orthodoxy of the Church." These were hidden years for Watchman Nee.

The eight long years of the Sino-Japanese War would finally come to an end. In August 1945 Japan surrendered unconditionally and an armistice with China was signed in September at Nanking. Brother Nee managed to return to Shanghai, but the assembly there was not ready to receive him at that time. Not until April of 1948 did he have the first opportunity of addressing the saints in Shanghai. In his first address, and referring to himself in the third person, Watchman said that he was like a widow who had to raise a family of children. Because of this she had to remarry, hoping thus that she might be able to feed all of them. Unexpectedly, however, all her children deserted her after the second marriage. He used this simile to explain how he had felt compelled to engage in the pharmaceutical business back in 1939.

At this point in his address Watchman broke down in tears. As he continued speaking, a great many of the saints present touched the life of Christ and felt the authority of the Spirit. The atmosphere of the gathering suddenly changed. All the past misunderstandings vanished without the need of further explanation. The floodgates of God's blessing were thus opened, with quite a revival having broken out in Shanghai. People rededicated their lives to God and gave their all for the Lord's interests.

Watchman Nee's burden at that time was now to be the training of workers. He was able to have two training sessions convened on Kuling Mountain for the young as well as potential workers. The first of these was held from June to the end of September 1948, and the second one began in the spring of 1949. Due to the Chinese civil war between the Nationalists and Communists having at one point come quite near to Foochow, this second session was moved down to the city itself, where it was successfully concluded.

On the 10th of April 1952 brother Nee was arrested by the Communist Chinese government and was eventually sentenced to twenty years imprisonment for his faith.

Through the messages delivered during this third stage of Watchman Nee's spiritual journey one is given to see something of the maturity of his spiritual life.

1: Excerpts from *The Release of the Spirit*

[28]Anyone who serves God will discover sooner or later that the great hindrance he has in the Lord's work is not others, but himself. He will discover that his outward man (soul) is not in harmony with his inward man (spirit). Both tend to go toward two opposite directions from each other. He will also sense the inability of his outward man to submit to the inner control of his regenerated spirit, received through the new birth. Thus, he is rendered incapable of obeying God's highest commands. He will quickly detect that his greatest difficulty lies in his outward man, which hinders him from using his spirit.

Many of God's servants are not able to do even the most elementary work. Ordinarily, they should be enabled by the exercise of their spirit to know God's Word, to discern the spiritual condition of another, to

---

[28] Watchman Nee, *The Release of the Spirit* (New York: Christian Fellowship Publishers, 2000), Ch. 1, pp. 11-12. This volume contains the text of the author's series of messages he delivered in late May 1948 in Foochow, southern China, on the theme of "The Breaking of the Outward Man unto the Release of the Spirit." The first Chinese language edition of the full text of these messages was published in May 1955 at Shanghai. It first appeared in English in 1965 in the United States, followed by several revised editions produced by the same publisher. Copyright transfer of the book to the current publisher occurred in 1999.—*Translator*

send forth God's messages under the anointing, and to receive God's illumination. Yet due to the distractions of the outward man, their spirit does not seem to function properly. It is basically because their outward man has never been dealt with. For this reason, excitement in revivals, pleading prayers, and zealous activities are but a waste of time. As we shall see, only one kind of basic dealing can enable man to be useful before God—*brokenness*.

[29]God desires firstly to *break* down the outward man, and secondly to *separate* it so that the inward man may no longer be entangled and mixed in with the outward man's activities. Or, we may simply say about this second point, God wants to divide our spirit from our soul.

How rare it is in these days to find an unmixed and pure spirit. Usually, whenever our spirit comes forth, it does so with our soul, because they are mixed. So another basic requirement in God's work is a *pure* spirit—not a powerful spirit. Those who neglect this will find their work damaged, though it is done with much power, due to the lack of the purity of spirit. Although they may truly possess the power of God, yet because their spirit is mixed with the natural powers of their soul, they are wrecking what they build. Let us see if we can understand how this is.

---

[29] *Ibid.*, Ch. 7, pp. 75-76.

[30]Since our greatest problem is this impure mixture, God must do a work in our lives beyond the breaking of our outward man. He must also purify and refine our outward man from the mixtures which God considers as impurities. While God is breaking our hard outer shell, He is also at the same time doing the work of refining. Thus, we see His *two-fold dealings* with us: *the breaking down of the outward man*, and *the dividing of it from the spirit*. The first is done through the discipline of the Holy Spirit, while the second is accomplished through the Spirit's revelation.

[31]Revelation *enables us to see what God sees*. All things are naked and laid bare before *Him*. The existence of any covering is something upon our own eyes, not God's. When God opens our eyes, we will truly know the intents of our heart and the deepest thoughts within us to the same degree as He himself knows them—this is revelation. And, we are as naked and laid bare before Him as we are now before ourselves—again, this is revelation. Revelation allows us to see exactly what our Lord sees.

---

[30] *Ibid.*, p. 76.
[31] *Ibid.*, pp. 83-84.

[32]For the breaking of the outward man, a full consecration is imperative. However, we must also understand that this crisis act of consecration alone will not solve the whole problem of service. Consecration is merely an expression of our unqualified willingness to be categorically in the hands of God. And it can take place in just a few minutes. Do not think God can do a quick work and finish His dealings with us in a short time. Although we are willing to offer ourselves completely to God, it is merely a start on our spiritual pilgrimage. It is like entering the gate. After the *gateway* of consecration, there is the long *pathway* of the discipline of the Holy Spirit. It takes an initial consecration plus the persistent discipline of the Holy Spirit to make us vessels prepared for the Master's use. However, without consecration, the Holy Spirit will encounter a difficult time in His discipline of our outer man. But remember that our consecration will never serve as a substitute for His discipline.

Here then is a vital distinction: Our consecration can only be according to our *limited* insight and understanding, but the Holy Spirit's discipline is according to God's own *unlimited* light. We really do not know to what extent our consecration should entail. Our light, though so limited, seems to us to be somewhat the brightest. But in God's view, when our light is compared with His own light, it will seem like pitch-blackness.

---

[32] *Ibid.*, Ch. 6, pp. 65-66.

Hence, the light of God's requirement exceeds far beyond our consecration under our diminished light. The discipline of the Holy Spirit, on the other hand, is parceled out to us according to God's own light. He knows our special need, and His Spirit orders our circumstances accordingly to bring about the breaking of the outward man. Remember this: The discipline of the Holy Spirit transcends far beyond our consecration.

2: Excerpts from *Spiritual Authority*

[33]There is no authority except from God; all authorities have been instituted by Him. By tracing all authorities back to their source we invariably end up with God. God is above all authorities, and all authorities are under Him. In touching God's authority we touch God himself. God's work basically is done not by power but by authority. He upholds all things by the powerful word of His authority, even as He created them by the same word. His word of command is authority. We cannot say how God's authority works; nevertheless, we know that He accomplishes everything by it.

Some Lessons on Obedience[34]

Sooner or later, those who serve God must meet authority in the universe, in society, in the home, in the church. How can one serve and obey God if he has never

---

[33] Watchman Nee, *Spiritual Authority* (New York: Christian Fellowship Publishers, 1972), Ch. 2, p. 22. This volume contains the text of a series of messages the author delivered during a lengthy Training Session for his fellow Christian workers held on Mount Kuling, Foochow, southern China, summer 1948. The contents of these messages were translated into English from the edited notes taken down by several Session attendees and published in 1972.—*Translator*

[34] *Ibid.*, pp. 24-25.

met the authority of God? This is more than a matter of teaching or doctrine, for a teaching can be abstract. Some think it is very difficult to know how to obey authority, but if we have met God the difficulty evaporates. There is no one who can obey God's authority without God's mercy being upon him. Let us therefore learn a few lessons:

1. Have a spirit of obedience.
2. Practice obedience. Some individuals are like savages who just cannot obey. But those who are trained do not feel bound no matter where they are placed. They can naturally live out obedience.
3. Learn to exercise delegated authority. He who works for God needs not only to learn to obey authority but also to learn how to be God's delegated authority in the church and in the home. Once you have learned how to be under God's authority, you will count yourself as nothing even after God entrusts you with much.

Submission Is Absolute, but Obedience Is Relative[35]

Submission is a matter of attitude, while obedience is a matter of conduct. Peter and John answered the Jewish religious council: "Whether it is right in the sight of God to hearken unto you rather than unto God, judge

---

[35] *Ibid.*, Ch. 11, pp. 107-108.

ye" (Acts 4.19). Their spirit was not rebellious, since they still submitted to those who were in authority. Obedience, however, cannot be absolute. Some authorities must be obeyed; while others should not be, especially in matters which touch upon Christian fundamentals—such as believing the Lord, preaching the gospel, and so forth. Children may make suggestions to their parents, yet they must not show an unsubmissive attitude. Submission ought to be absolute. Sometimes obedience is submission, whereas at other times an inability to obey may still be submission. Even when making a suggestion, we should maintain an attitude of submission.

To Be Great, One Must Be a Servant[36]

The authority whom God appoints must have a spiritual background—he must drink the cup, that is, absolutely obey God's will; and he must receive the baptism, that is, accept death in order to release life. He must also not have any intention of exercising authority; on the contrary, he must be prepared to serve as the servant and slave of all. In other words, he possesses spiritual ground on the one hand and the spirit of humility on the other. Because he does not seek to be authority God can use him as one. It is irrelevant to talk about authority if the cup is not drunk and the baptism

[36] *Ibid.*, Ch. 18, pp. 175-176.

not received. To one who is truly humble and considers himself unfit for anything except to be servant of all, to that one the Lord announces that he may be great.

The condition for authority is consequently a sense of incompetency and unworthiness. From the Bible we can conclude that God has never used a proud soul. The moment a person becomes proud, at that moment he is laid aside by God. His hidden pride sooner or later will be revealed through his words, for words do not cease to leak out. At the future judgment seat of God even the humble will be greatly surprised. And if that be true, how much more shall be the horror of the proud on that day! We must sense our incompetency, because God only uses the useless. Polite diplomacy is not the thing here; rather is it having a sincere sense that we are but unprofitable servants. Though we have tended the flock and tilled the field, yet in coming back we still acknowledge ourselves as unprofitable servants. We do not forget to stand on the ground of a servant. God never entrusts His authority to the self-righteous and the self-competent. Let us reject pride, learn to be humble and gentle, and never speak for ourselves. Let us learn to know ourselves in the light of God.

3: Excerpt from *Spiritual Discernment*

[37]When I try to discern the condition of another's spirit, how do I know that his spirit is wrong and mine is right? How do I conclude that his spirit has not been released? Is my own spirit up to standard? If my spirit is below standard, then I cannot make the right judgment. It is very wrong for many who judge people while they themselves have not been judged. People usually judge according to knowledge, but we must judge by the spirit. We need first of all to have no confidence in our spirit. Like a balance with different measures, our spirit itself must first be adjusted or corrected. Therefore, let us not place confidence in ourselves too early. The only reason we may judge is because we have first been judged by God. The way God trains us for future service is to let us learn first through dealings. The sensitivity of my spirit is based on my experience of when I am dealt with by God. If my spirit is released and God says it was wrong and I learn from that experience, only then can I say wrong to

---

[37] Watchman Nee, *Spiritual Discernment* (New York: Christian Fellowship Publishers, 2010), Ch. 11, pp. 45-47. This is a collection of notes of various messages given by the author during the spring of 1949. These notes were set down in Chinese by several who were present to hear the author speak. They were acquired by the Publishers several years ago and were subsequently translated and published in English.—*Translator*

my brethren when their spirits come forth in like manner. No one can judge out of knowledge. Objective judgment is useless here, only subjective discernment acquired through discipline is useful. I can judge only according to what I myself have been judged by God. My judgment can never surpass God's judgment of me. Otherwise, it will be objective in nature. The more we receive the discipline of the Holy Spirit and are broken, the better we can discern. The legitimacy of my judgment depends on the discipline I have received. Because I have been disciplined, I use the light acquired thereby to judge others. This is God's judgment. There is no self hidden behind nor personal feeling involved. In case there is something in me that has not been judged, I cannot judge or discern when this very thing appears in others—with the result that I allow that sin to remain in my brother as well as in me.

Some may learn yet such learning may not be thorough enough. Judgment or discernment comes not from knowledge, cleverness or mind. It comes from what I have gone through myself. Since God has broken something in my life, I am able to judge. Therefore, let us not try to escape from discipline and personal dealing lest we cannot deal with other people. We need to learn deeply so that we may be useful. Whatever lesson you have learned from discipline or revelation, that very thing you will store in your spirit. He who is broken most is the richest for ministering to others. What is meant by ministry, your ministry? It means that you use what you have learned and stored in your spirit to help others. This is ministry. Let there be prayers asking the Lord to increase His judgment in me that I might be enriched, that I may appreciate what is beautiful and recognize what is problematic. The Lord will deal with my spirit daily till it becomes dependable.

THE FINAL STAGE OF MY SPIRITUAL JOURNEY (1952-1972)

From His Arrest and Imprisonment to His Death

In April of 1952 Watchman Nee was ordered by the Communist Chinese government to go to Manchuria. There he was arrested by the Department of Public Safety on the 10th of April. He was imprisoned in Harbin. No one knew what had happened to him for the government kept everything secret. On 21 June 1956 Watchman appeared before the High Court in Shanghai and was given the maximum sentence of fifteen years imprisonment. He was to serve this entire sentence in the First Municipal Prison in Shanghai.

By April 1967 brother Nee had served his fifteen years, but he was not released. The authorities had attempted to force him to renounce his faith but the Lord was dearer to him than was his freedom. And thus his sentence was extended another five years. He was secretly transferred from the Municipal Prison to Tsing-Tong Labor Farm in Tsing-Po County, a suburb of Shanghai. Then, suddenly, in January of 1970 Watchman was transferred to a stricter labor camp called White Mao Mountain Farm in far-off Kuang-Teh County, Anhwei Province.

On 12 April 1972 he completed his twenty-year prison term. There was every expectation that he would be released. For unknown reasons, in May of 1972 the sixty-eight-year-old Watchman was removed from the collective prison camp to a private cell at the foot of the mountain.

On the first day of June 1972 brother Nee's sister-in-law received a telegram from the White Mao Mountain Farm Labor Camp that simply read: "Watchman Nee died of sickness at the foot of the mountain."

These twenty long years of imprisonment were years of silence. Watchman Nee was not able to minister with word but only by deed. For it is known that he maintained a good testimony to the Lord by the few letters which he was allowed to send to his relatives, plus a note which he left behind in his cell.

Last letter written on 22 April 1972 to his sister-in-law: [38]

"Elder sister Ping-Tseng:

I have received your letter of 7 April and learned from it that you have not received mine which acknowledged the receipt of each parcel you sent me. All the things you mentioned in your letter I have received. I am most grateful to you.

You know my physical condition. It is a chronic disease, an organic disease. When attacks come, they are most painful. At times of recession the disease is still with me. The difference is in the degree of activity, not in the sense of recovery. The summer has arrived. More exposure to sunlight may change a little the color of the skin, but it cannot affect the illness. However, please do not worry, because I maintain my joy. I hope you will also take good care of yourself. May your heart be filled with joy.

Wishing you well,

Shu-Tsu
April 22

---

[38] This final extant letter of the author's was translated into English and published in "A Sketch of the Author's Life" in Watchman Nee, *The Finest of the Wheat*, 2 vols (New York: Christian Fellowship Publishers, 1992-1993), Vol. I, pp. 30-31.—*Translator*

Signed Note found beneath his cell's bed pillow with several lines in large letters written by Watchman Nee's shaking hand: [39]

Christ is the Son of God, who died to atone for men's sins and who rose on the third day. This is the greatest fact in the universe. I believe in Christ and die.

Signed,
Watchman Nee

[39] *Ibid.*, p. 32.

OTHER TITLES AVAILABLE
From Christian Fellowship Publishers

By Watchman Nee

The Basic Lesson Series
Vol. 1 - A Living Sacrifice
Vol. 2 - The Good Confession
Vol. 3 - Assembling Together
Vol. 4 - Not I, But Christ
Vol. 5 - Do All to the Glory of God
Vol. 6 - Love One Another

Aids to "Revelation"
Back to the Cross
A Balanced Christian Life
The Better Covenant
The Body of Christ: A Reality
The Character of God's Workman
Christ the Sum of All Spiritual Things
The Church and the Work – 3 Vols
"Come, Lord Jesus"
The Communion of the Holy Spirit
The Finest of the Wheat – Vol. 1
The Finest of the Wheat – Vol. 2
From Faith to Faith
From Glory to Glory
Full of Grace and Truth – Vol. 1
Full of Grace and Truth – Vol. 2
Gleanings in the Fields of Boaz
The Glory of His Life
God's Plan and the Overcomers
God's Work
Gospel Dialogue
Grace for Grace
Heart to Heart Talks
Interpreting Matthew
Journeying towards the Spiritual
The King and the Kingdom of Heaven
The Latent Power of the Soul
Let Us Pray
The Life That Wins
The Lord My Portion
The Messenger of the Cross
The Ministry of God's Word
The Mystery of Creation
My Spiritual Journey
Powerful According to God
Practical Issues of This Life
The Prayer Ministry of the Church
The Release of the Spirit
Revive Thy Work
The Salvation of the Soul
The Secret of Christian Living
Serve in Spirit
The Spirit of Judgment
The Spirit of the Gospel
The Spirit of Wisdom and Revelation
Spiritual Authority
Spiritual Exercise
Spiritual Discernment
Spiritual Knowledge
The Spiritual Man
Spiritual Reality or Obsession
Take Heed
The Testimony of God
Whom Shall I Send?
The Word of the Cross
Worship God
Ye Search the Scriptures

ORDER FROM: 11515 Allecingie Pkwy Richmond, VA 23235
www.c-f-p.com

OTHER TITLES AVAILABLE
From Christian Fellowship Publishers

By Stephen Kaung

The "God Has Spoken" Series
Seeing Christ in the Old Testament, Part One
Seeing Christ in the Old Testament, Part Two
Seeing Christ in the New Testament

Discipled to Christ
The Gymnasium of Christ
In the Footsteps of Christ
The Songs of Degrees – *Meditations on Fifteen Psalms*
The Splendor of His Ways – *Seeing the Lord's End in Job*
New Covenant Living & Ministry